The Yacht Racing Rules Today

BILL BENTSEN

The Yacht Racing Rules Today

ILLUSTRATED WITH
DRAWINGS BY
TED BRENNAN

DODD, MEAD & COMPANY
New York

Copyright © 1974 by Bill Bentsen
All rights reserved
No part of this book may be reproduced in any form
without permission in writing from the publisher

ISBN: 0-396-06927-4
Library of Congress Catalog Card Number: 74-2599
Printed in the United States of America

To racing sailors everywhere

Preface

We take on new interests for various reasons, but sometimes a particular experience is the beginning. My interest in the Racing Rules goes back to a protest hearing during the 1948 intercollegiate Thanksgiving regatta at Belmont Harbor, Chicago. I was the protestee, and in due course was disqualified. The details are now long forgotten, but what still remains is the image of the chairman of the Protest Committee taking special pains to get the facts without undue hurry, and then, following his decision (I think he was a one-member committee), taking even greater pains to explain to me how the rule applied and where I had gone wrong. Soon afterward I decided that racing would be more fun if I could avoid running afoul of the rules. Moreover, a clear understanding of the rules would help avoid defeat at the protest table. I began to study the rules and found it a fascinating hobby in itself. Perhaps you will too.

My friends Sam Merrick, Dick Rose, and Allen T. Klots, Jr. of Dodd, Mead have offered several helpful suggestions, and I want to thank them here.

BILL BENTSEN

Contents

Preface		vii
Designations Used by Appeals Committees and in This Book		x
1	Before We Begin	1
2	The Basics	9
3	Beyond the Basics—Part I	30
4	Beyond the Basics—Part II	68
5	The Race: Rules and Tactics	112
6	When You Go to Court	129
7	Maintaining Your Rules Knowledge	143
	Appendix A. The 1973 Yacht Racing Rules of the International Yacht Racing Union, Parts I, IV, and VI	146
	Appendix B. Changes in the 1969 Racing Rules, Parts I and IV	166
	Appendix C. The Iceboat Racing Rules	170
	Appendix D. Mailing Addresses of the Four Major Racing Unions and Associations: the IYRU, the RYA, the CYA, and the NAYRU	174
	Appendix E. A List of IYRU Cases and Other Appeals Cited	175
	Index	178

Designations Used by Appeals Committees and in This Book

S   Starboard tack
P   Port tack
L   Leeward
W   Windward
A   Ahead
B   Behind
I   Inside (or Intervening)
O   Outside

1

Before We Begin

Sailboat racing is both a sport and a game, and in games the rules are important. Racing skill and knowledge of the rules do not go hand in hand; there are first-rate sailors who know only the basics of the rules, and there are rules experts who achieve only moderate racing success. This absence of any close relationship between racing success and rules expertise suggests two rather different yet equally sensible approaches to the rules. You might decide to learn only the most important rules and then race hard but cautiously when near other boats. Or, you may decide that a thorough knowledge of all the rules is important, so that you can feel confident about what you can and cannot do in tight situations on the race course.

Both these approaches work, and this book is for both

2 – The Yacht Racing Rules Today

types of sailor. We will take basic principles first—there are only a handful—and then move into all the right-of-way rules in detail. The book's objective is to explain what each rule says, what it means, when it most likely will apply, and how to use it.

The Book's Plan

The next chapter begins your rules learning. In it, we will look at the basic rules, then sail a simplified race to see when these basic rules usually come into play. In later chapters all the right-of-way rules come under our microscope, along with the more tricky aspects of the definitions. We will also discover some basic principles that appear frequently in the rules. The most useful appeals cases are included, taken from those of the International Yacht Racing Union (IYRU), the North American Yacht Racing Union (NAYRU), and Britain's Royal Yachting Association (RYA). The appeals used here have been selected from IYRU Cases 1–65, NAYRU Appeals 1–159, and the RYA Racing Appeals Cases from 1962 through 1973. North American readers will want the NAYRU Appeals book as a reference, although it is not necessary in reading this book.

Following this in-depth look at the rules, we will take a second sail around the course, this time looking at groups of rules in action and seeing how the rules affect tactics. After that, preparation for protest meetings is discussed. We close with some suggestions on how you can stay current on your rules knowledge and even become your own rules expert. The appendices include the complete text of Parts I, IV, and VI of the IYRU Rules; a summary of changes in Parts I and IV since the 1969 edition; the iceboat racing rules; mailing addresses for the IYRU, NAYRU, RYA, and CYA (Canadian

Yachting Association); and a list of rules cases cited. An index by rule numbers supplements a traditional index.

Yacht Racing: The Game

Any game has certain objects. Winning the game depends on the player's ability to apply different skills, and there are different "types of play" that can work. Racing sailboats is no exception. The object is clear; in individual races we want to cross the finish line first, and in a regatta or a season's series we want the best point score. The skills to be mastered make sailing the wonderful sport and game that it is: everything from physical prowess to technical knowledge comes into play. Helmsmanship, tactical judgement, crew organization, wind and current prediction, tuning of rig and sails, and use of the racing rules are only the start of a lengthier list. No one sailor masters all these skills; the world's best are successful only because they have mastered more of them than have the rest of us.

Later we will see how the rules affect tactical decisions, a solid reason in itself for spending time to learn the rules. But the rules play another, more significant, role: they help *define* the game itself. Just as lines on a tennis court or restrictions on dribbling a basketball define those games, yacht racing is defined by rules that prescribe the playing area (the sailing instructions specify the course), the equipment that can be used (class rules limit the boat and other equipment), and contestants' actions during the play itself (the racing rules stipulate rights and obligations, most importantly the right-of-way relationships between boats). In thus helping to define the game the racing rules serve another objective: equity, or fairness between contestants.

4 – The Yacht Racing Rules Today

The rules have a third function also—one that historically has often been considered the exclusive purpose—safety. By prescribing right-of-way, the rules try to keep boats apart. Avoiding damage to equipment and injury to contestants is a worthy objective for any game's rules, and when the game is played on the changing surface of sometimes-dangerous water, with movable objects that themselves contain the contestants, safety becomes especially important. Yet the hazards of racing have steadily diminished as boats have become smaller and more maneuverable. Nowadays, the rules are designed not only for safety, but also for tactical interest, and fairness.

Knowing the rules is important for all these reasons. When it comes to racing success, the rules are sometimes almost inconsequential and other times are critically important. One day, you may get off the starting line with the gun, moving fast, and manage to sail the entire race without encountering anyone at close quarters. Another time, you will be caught in a jam at a leeward mark with boats inside and outside you. It is such days that make learning the rules seem especially important.

The Rule-Making Process

All the rules, including the right-of-way rules, are the product of a continuing process in which ideas from sailors and race officials are channeled through national sailing organizations to the International Yacht Racing Union, which is composed of these national organizations. The Racing Rules Committee of the IYRU reviews the rules annually, and every fourth year produces a new rulebook. Each "national authority," as it is called, such as the North American

Yacht Racing Union, which has this authority for the United States, the Canadian Yachting Association, and the Royal Yachting Association, then adopts the rules for home use. Modifications may be made to accommodate national preferences, but not to Parts I or IV. Thus the right-of-way rules are identical everywhere.

The Language of the Rules

Throughout the rules, we will find a variety of statements. Some say what you may do, some what you must not do, some what you must do, and some what you need not do. One or two seem nearly useless. Some are only procedural. Others state the "onus of satisfying the race committee"—when a contestant can be tentatively presumed guilty and therefore must take extra pains to convince the committee otherwise. Some statements are crystal-clear, such as rule 36's "A port-tack yacht shall keep clear of a starboard-tack yacht." Others use vague words and phrases such as "substantial," "normal," "with advantage," "seriously," "reasonable," and "vicinity." We will see that much of this vagueness is harmless, but some of it can be crucial indeed. Yet most all of it is unavoidable, in the difficult business of building a good set of rules.

If a really thorough understanding of the rules is your goal, shoot for this as your ideal: to know them so well that you instinctively know your rights when encountering other boats. If you can get close to this ideal, then you won't need to think about the rules while racing. You can concentrate on sailing fast, and in the right direction, using the rules, without effort, only when you have a tactical objective in mind.

The Rulebook: A Once-over Look

The rulebook is divided into six chapters, including definitions of terms, race-management details, general prerace requirements of contestants, the right-of-way rules, other rules that apply while racing, and complaint procedures—for protests, hearings, and appeals. At the end there are appendices, some of which bear on the racing rules. We will concentrate almost exclusively on Part I, "Definitions," and Part IV, "Sailing Rules When Yachts Meet," although the chapter "When You Go to Court" includes the main points in Part VI, "Protests, Disqualifications, and Appeals."

Open your own rulebook now. Notice that the definitions require only two pages; the rules of Part IV another seven and a half. Mastering fewer than ten pages should not seem too formidable a challenge, although I won't claim it is especially easy either. Within Part IV's rules, however, there are only a few of major importance, and these can easily be summarized in a general way:

1. When on port tack, keep clear of boats on starboard.
2. When to windward of boats on the same tack, keep clear.
3. When behind boats on the same tack, keep clear.
4. When overlapped with inside boats at marks or obstructions, give them room.
5. When changing course, allow other boats time and space to keep clear.

These are the "basics" we will examine more closely in the next chapter. The actual wording of the rules is more precise, and therefore more accurate than the five statements above. There are some important exceptions, too. However, if you keep these five ideas in mind you will avoid trouble on the course most of the time.

In this book the rules are discussed in groups, according to their importance, and not in the order they are numbered in the rulebook. When you want to read about a particular rule, use the index to locate its explanation.

The definitions, found in Part I of the rulebook, are not discussed separately. They come into our discussion only when we look at a rule. You will want to read the definitions as they come up; any word in boldface type in a rule is a definition. As you read this book keep your own rulebook nearby.

The Appeals

Unfortunately, it must be said that not all the rules are in the rulebook. Some few are to be found only in the appeals. In a small number of these cases the decision rendered has in effect created new law. We will come to these instances when we look at specific rules. Generally, however, the appeals are decisions about the meaning of the rules, usually arising from actual protest hearings, but sometimes from questions asked by clubs. They vary widely in their value but the most useful ones are useful indeed. Some of them have been given special prominence by the IYRU; these have been culled from British, North American, Russian, Italian, Canadian, and Dutch appeals records, and then published together. They can be considered to be more important than other national appeals. Technically, one country's own set of appeals ranks higher than appeals decided elsewhere, but as a practical matter all appeals are valuable in learning the rules and preparing protests, and the appeals of the NAYRU and the RYA are respected by protest committees around the world. In this book, the appeals are not reviewed in detail, but when a case helps explain a rule or verifies an interpretation it is identified and discussed.

Your Learning Viewpoint

Try not to make learning the rules any harder than necessary. Follow these suggestions:

1. Read the *words* themselves. Don't deal with sloganlike phrases as substitutes; they can mislead you.
2. Don't use your own definitions for words. The boldface words in the rules are defined in Part I. A dictionary can be helpful for some of the others.
3. When considering an actual case, avoid making up your mind about who is right until you take a fresh look at the rulebook. Do this no matter how well you *think* you understand the rules.
4. Don't accumulate ideas on how the rules are interpreted from cases you hear about. For good solid case study, stick with the appeals. Read local decisions and decide whether you agree with them. Sometimes they are wrong.

The essential idea is to rely on the rules themselves along with solid interpretation from valid decisions, and to apply your thinking with as little prejudgment or bias as possible.

Now, on to "the basics."

2

The Basics

When on port tack, keep clear of boats on starboard. This is the first of our five basic rules. In the rule book it is labeled a "Fundamental Rule" and is rule 36, the only rule under the heading "Opposite Tack Rules":

> A **port-tack** yacht shall keep clear of a **starboard-tack** yacht.

Notice the words in bold face type; this means a word has a meaning stated in Part I, "Definitions."

The idea behind rule 36 is simple, although some of the situations in which it applies can be surprising at first. You may encounter starboard tackers like this:

10 – The Yacht Racing Rules Today

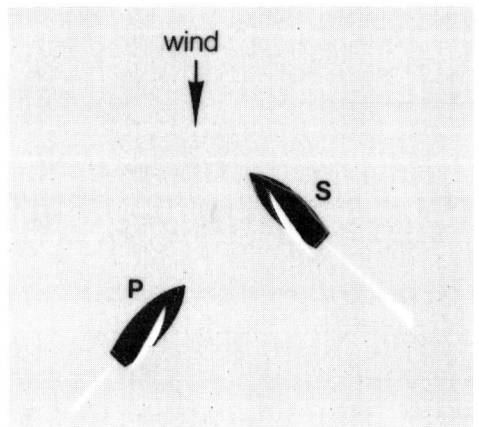

like this:

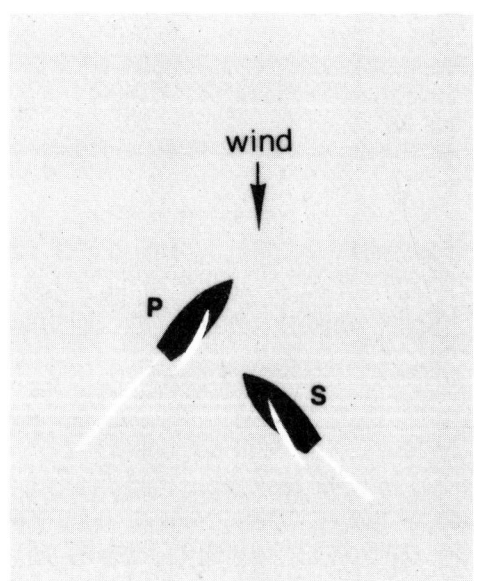

like this:

The Basics – 11

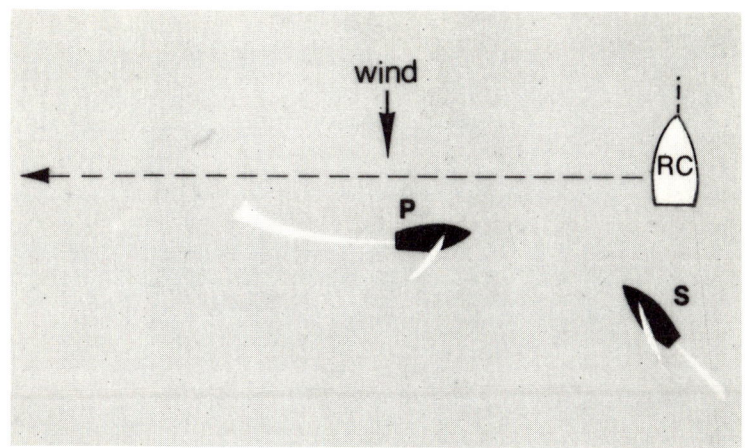

or like this:

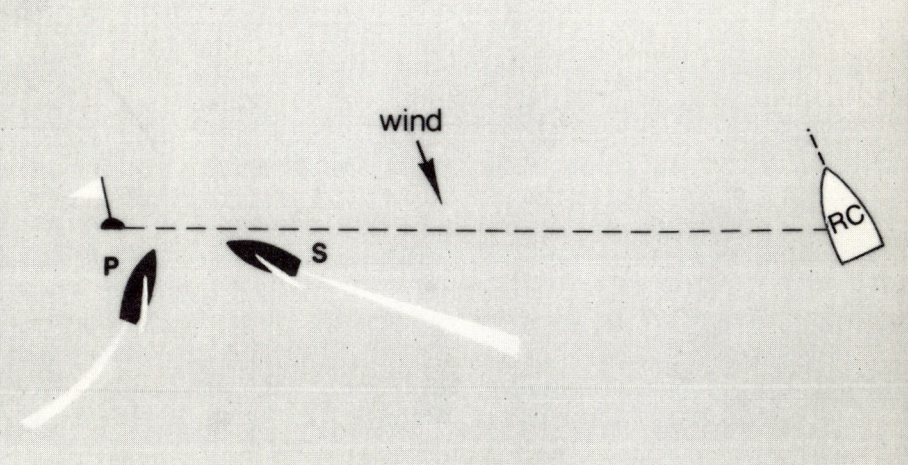

Also, you may experience these encounters: when running downwind, starboard tackers may be behind:

12 – The Yacht Racing Rules Today

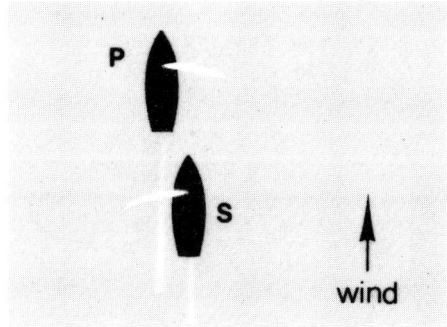

or ahead:

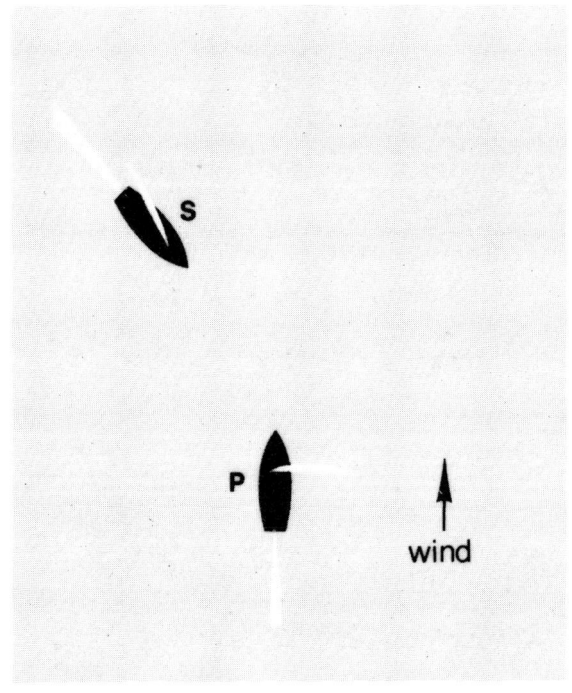

or both:

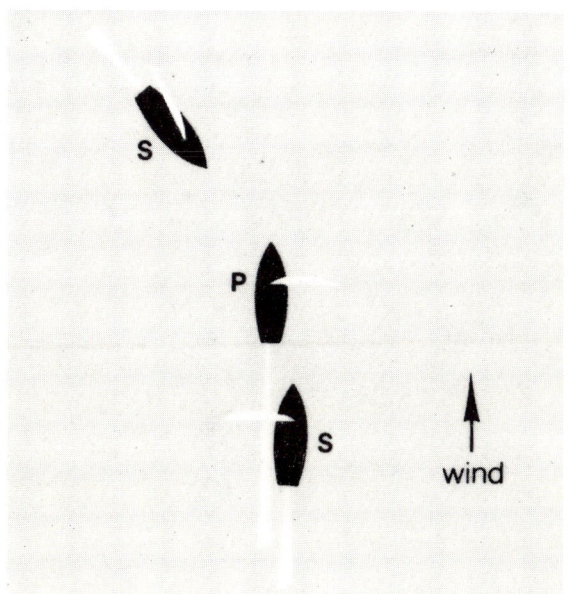

"Keep clear" means don't hit the other boat, but more than that it means stay out of her way. The rules are for changing situations, as boats move toward or away from each other, so it is important to anticipate where other boats are going.

The starboard-tack boat is not free to do just as she pleases, however, and sometimes loses her right-of-way or has it limited in some way. Rounding marks, for example, an outside starboard tacker must give room to an inside port tacker:

14 – The Yacht Racing Rules Today

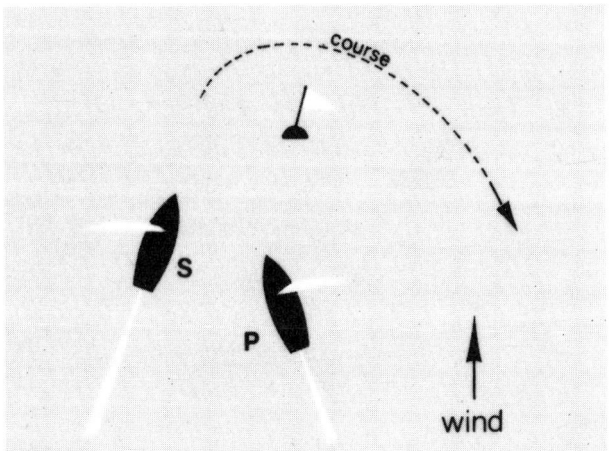

Or, when an inside starboard tacker must jibe to go toward the next mark, she must do it instead of hindering an outside port-tack boat:

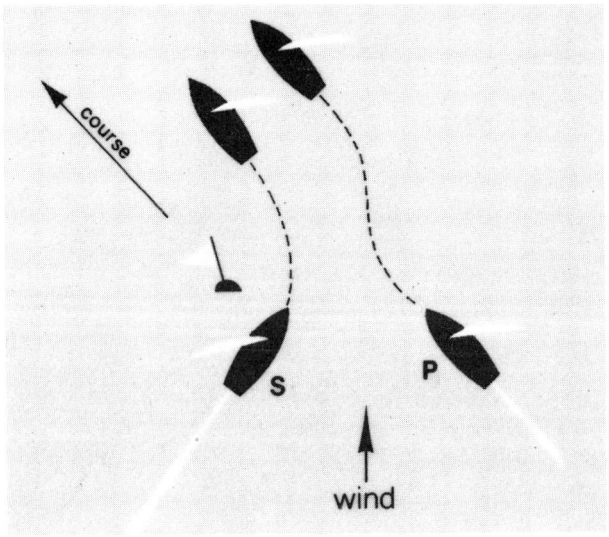

We will consider mark-rounding rules again later. For now, remember that starboard tackers almost always have right-of-way.

The second basic is: when to windward of boats on the same tack, keep clear (rule 37.1):

A **windward yacht** shall keep clear of a **leeward yacht.**

You can encounter leeward boats before the start:

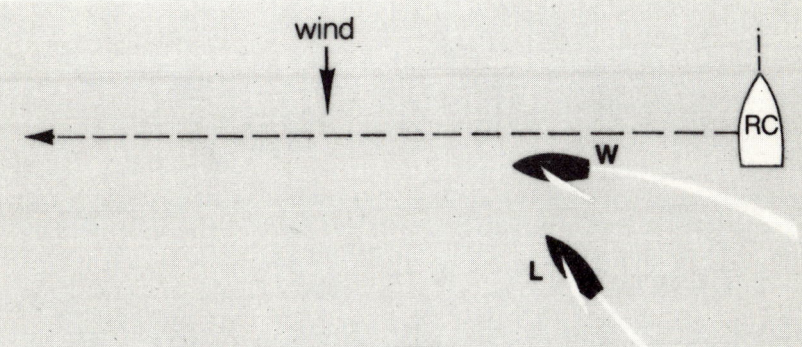

on windward legs:

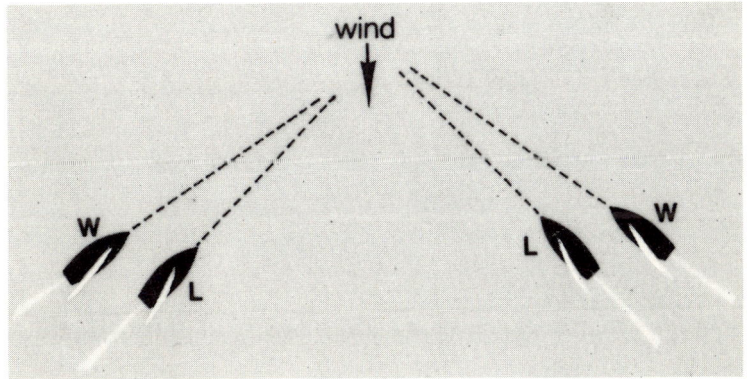

16 – The Yacht Racing Rules Today

on reaches:

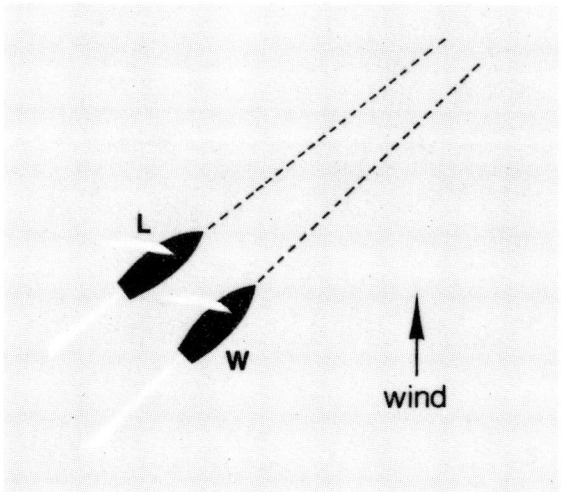

or on the run:

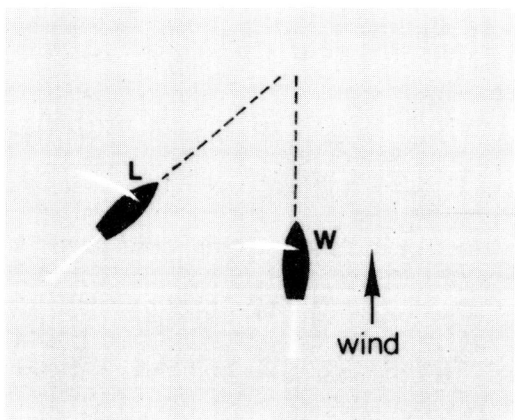

Watch for leeward boats just after rounding windward marks:

The Basics – 17

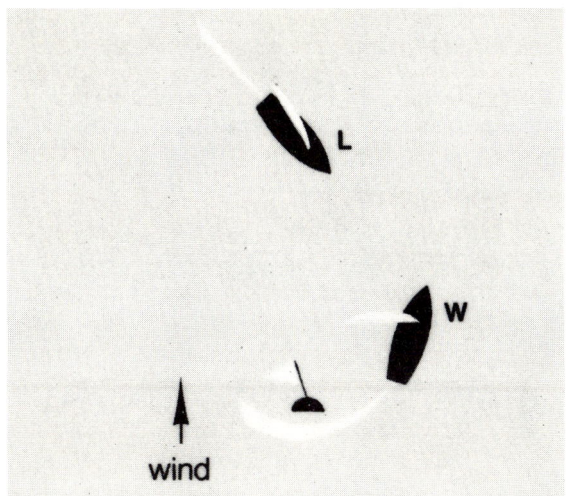

However, when overlapped at marks, outside leeward boats give room. This is the major exception to our second basic:

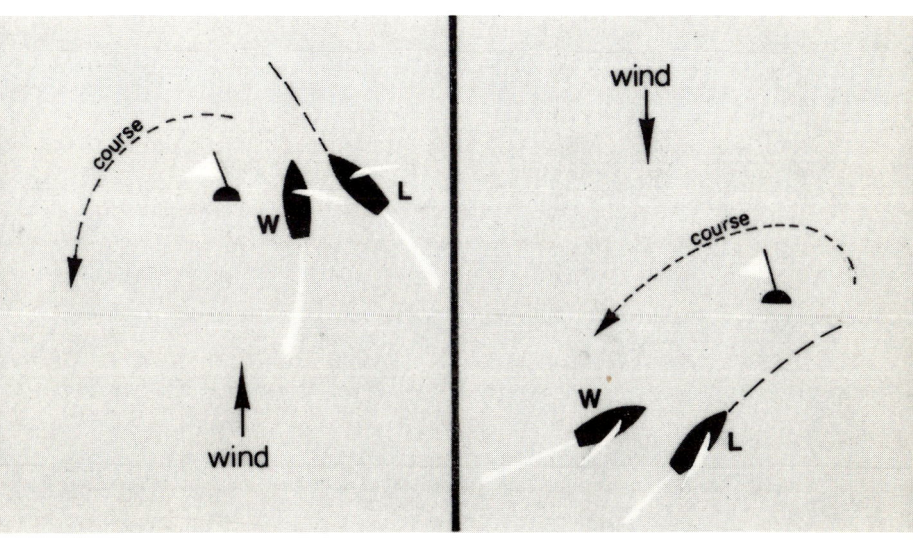

18 – The Yacht Racing Rules Today

The windward-leeward rule applies more often than some may think. It even allows boats without luffing rights to luff, as we will see later. For now, when to windward of other boats, give them right-of-way.

The third basic is: when behind boats on the same tack, keep clear. This is rule 37.2:

> A yacht **clear astern** shall keep clear of a yacht **clear ahead.**

Watch out for boats ahead of you near the starting line:

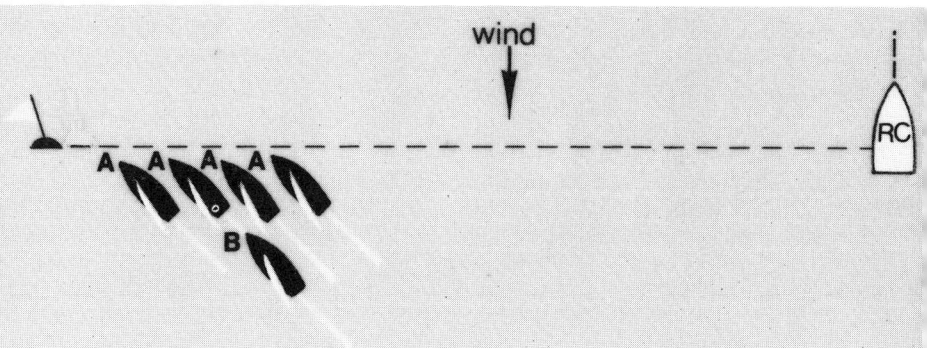

on windward legs:

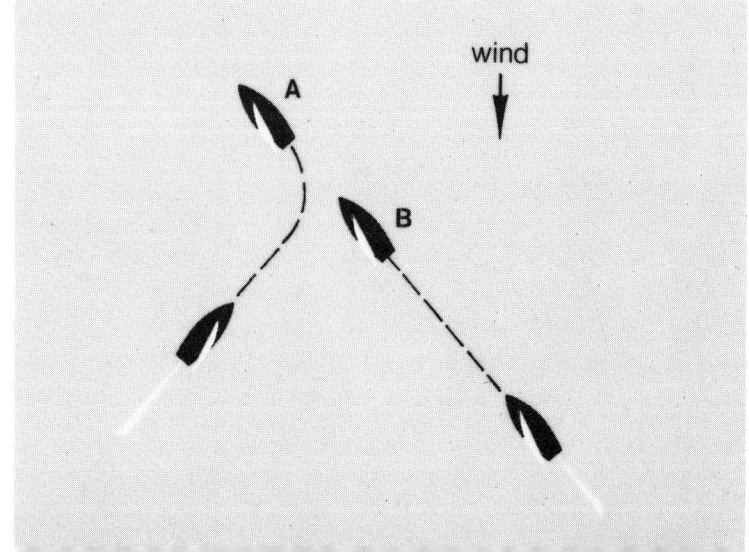

The Basics – 19

reaches:

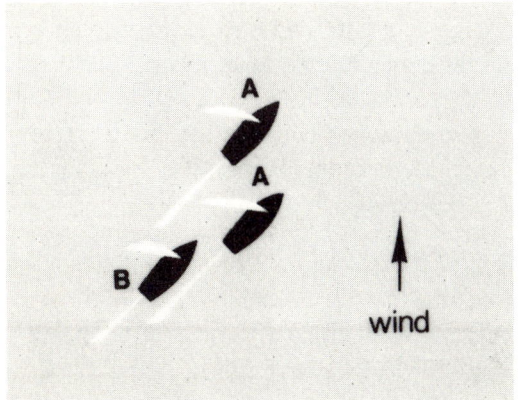

or runs:

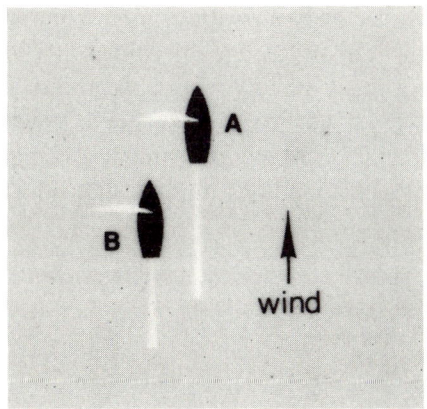

But remember: rule 37.2 applies only to boats on the same tack. If the overtaking boat is on starboard (see page 12), and the boat ahead on port, the boat ahead keeps clear.

Keeping clear of boats ahead is no problem when everyone is moving at about the same speed. It can be a real problem at crowded starts when boats ahead are creeping up to the line, or on windy days when a boat behind, sailing on a reach or run, gets a good ride on a wave. Just remember, if on the same tack and astern, keep clear.

The first three basics have already partly explained the fourth: when overlapped with inside boats at marks or obstructions, give them room. Rule 42, sometimes an exception to the first three basics, says it this way:

When yachts . . . are about to round or pass a **mark** on the same required side, . . . or an **obstruction** on the same side. . . . An outside yacht shall give each yacht **overlapping** her on the inside room to round or pass. . .

The complete rule is lengthy and somewhat complex, but the core idea is quite simple. It is essentially an attempt to ensure fairness as well as saftey: one boat should not be allowed to gain an advantage by squeezing out another, if they arrive at a mark or obstruction at about the same time. This explains why a starboard tacker, or a leeward boat, must give way at marks (look again at pages 14 and 17).

Mark-roundings sometimes happen like this:

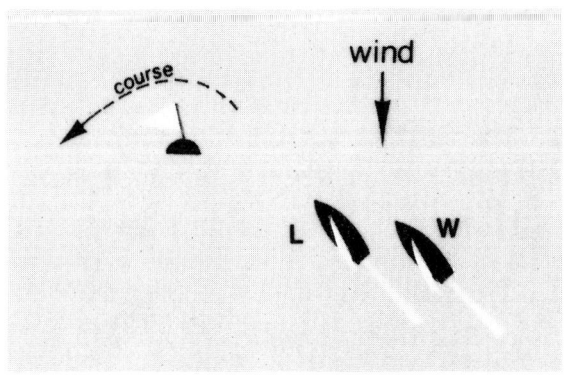

The Basics – 21

like this:

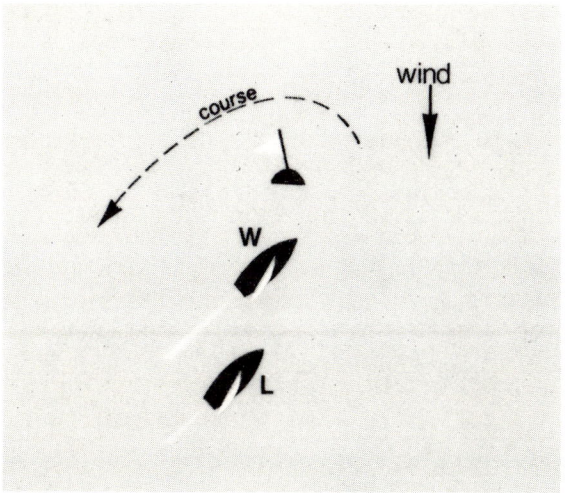

or like this:

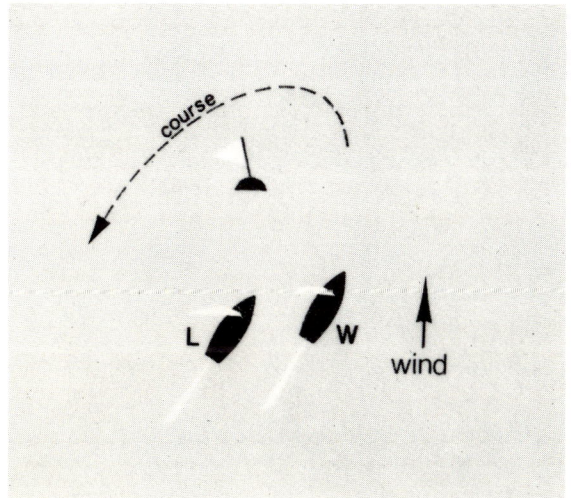

At leeward marks, encounters can occur between boats coming from quite different directions:

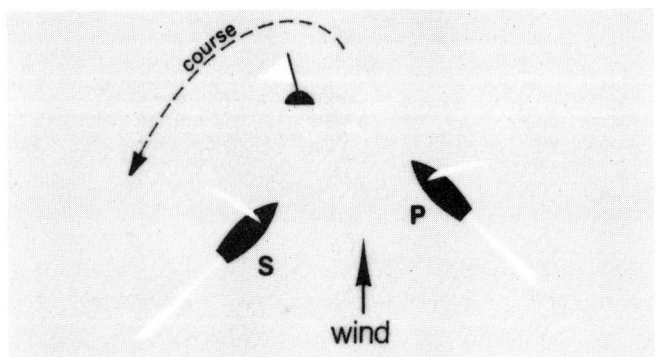

The definition entitled "Clear Ahead and Clear Astern; Overlap" explains how boats on quite different courses can be overlapped. If one boat is ahead of an imaginary perpendicular line drawn through the other's aftmost point, they are overlapped. Each of these boats is overlapped with all the others:

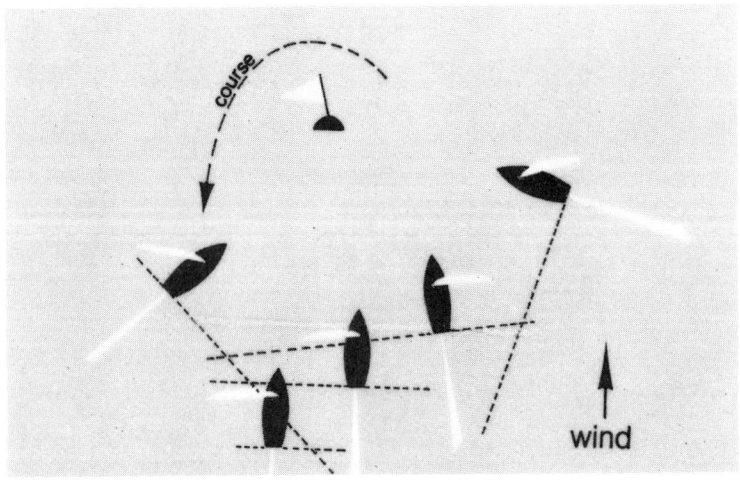

The Basics – 23

We will look later at some interesting cases involving rule 42 and the niceties of the overlap definition, but for now things can remain simple: when near a mark or obstruction, and outside other boats, give room to these boats if a line across the stern of your boat would pass through or behind any part of them.

The last basic is expressed in three rules, 41.2, 35, and 34. The principle is: when changing course, allow other boats time and space to keep clear. Rule 41.2 says:

A yacht shall neither **tack** nor **jibe** into a position which will give her right of way unless she does so far enough from a yacht **on a tack** to enable this yacht to keep clear . . .

Tacking and jibing are only two kinds of course changes, but are especially important because they involve changing tack, and because both of them usually result in different rights, under the rules.

The two other rules expressing this basic both apply to the right-of-way boat. Rule 35 says:

. . . a right-of-way yacht which does not hail before or when making an alteration of course which may not be foreseen by the other yacht may be disqualified . . .

The importance of hailing is that by warning the other boat of your intentions, you give her time to prepare for your maneuver.

Rule 34 is a general prohibition against right-of-way boats changing course in such a way as to interfere with other boats that are meeting their obligations to keep clear:

. . . the right-of-way yacht shall not so alter course as to prevent the other yacht from keeping clear, or so as to obstruct her . . .

24 – The Yacht Racing Rules Today

The thought behind this rule is essentially one of fairness. If you are keeping clear of another boat as required, then the other boat should not be permitted to maneuver so as to make your job unnecessarily difficult or impossible.

These three rules are somewhat more involved than we have seen so far, and have a few exceptions as we will see later. For the time being, however, just remember our fifth basic. Here are some typical encounters where it applies.

Going to windward, you may decide to tack into a port-starboard situation giving you right-of-way:

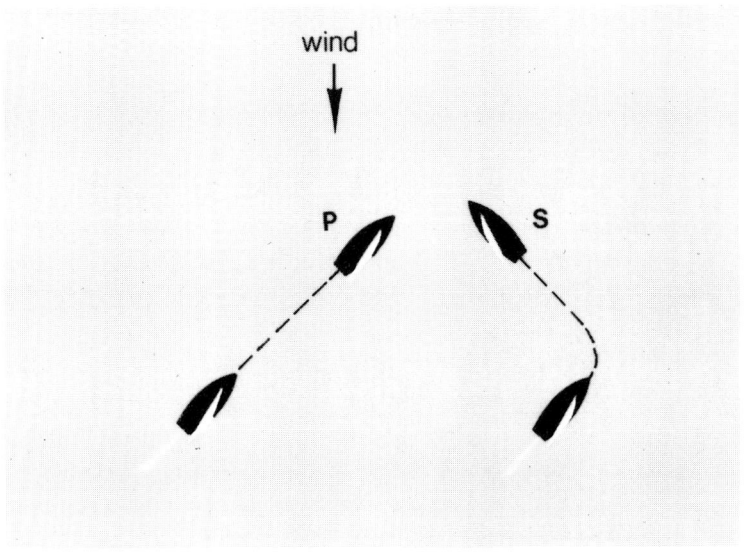

Before tacking, be sure there is room for you to tack without the other boat having to begin to keep clear of you until your tack has been completed (rule 41.2; also read carefully the definition of tacking). Then, hail (rule 35).

Or, you may plan to tack into position ahead and to leeward of another boat:

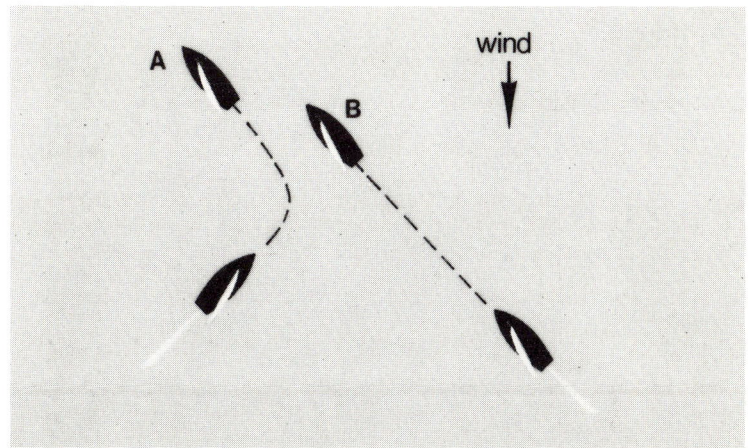

Rule 41.2 applies here, too. Before tacking, rule 36 requires you, on port, to keep clear of the starboard-tack boat. After you tack, you will have right-of-way as leeward boat (rule 37.1). But in between, heed rule 41.2. You must finish your tack before the other boat is required to take avoiding action.

A port tacker may be crossing ahead of you, on a windward leg:

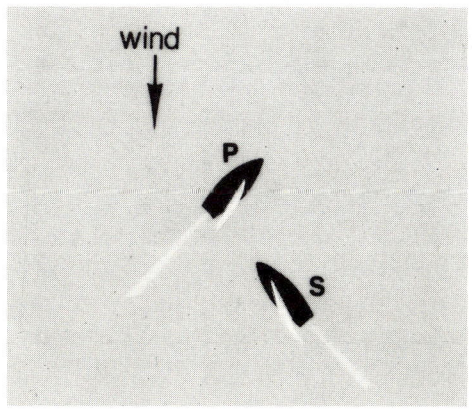

Don't luff up to hit her:

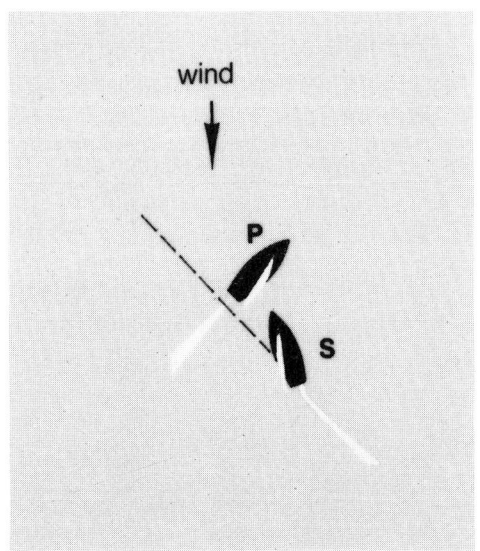

Rule 34 prohibits it.

To review, these five basics express the most important rules of Part IV:

1. When on port tack, keep clear of boats on starboard (rule 36).
2. When to windward of boats on the same tack, keep clear (rule 37.1).
3. When behind boats on the same tack, keep clear (rule 37.2).
4. When overlapped with inside boats at marks or obstructions, give them room (rule 42.1(a)(i)).
5. When changing course, allow other boats time and space to keep clear (rules 34, 35, and 41.2).

Notice which definitions have come into play in the wording of these rules. Take a minute to look again at the explanations in Part I of Tacking, Jibing, On a Tack, Clear Astern and Clear Ahead, Overlap, Leeward and Windward.

When do these basic rules apply during a typical race? Let's sail a simple triangular course, finishing with an extra windward leg.

At the five-minute signal the rules apply in earnest (read rule 31 and the definition of racing), and within this final period before starting you will encounter more boats sailing in more different directions than at any other time during the race. Starboard tack gives you right-of-way over port-tack boats, but much of the time you will be on port tack yourself. Keep a sharp lookout at all times; when on starboard don't make sudden moves that obstruct port tackers, and when on port stay well clear of starboard boats. On either tack, watch for boats behind and to leeward. Just before the start, be on starboard, and if you are not close-hauled be especially watchful for boats to leeward, sailing higher than you are. Starting marks are an exception to the principle of giving room to inside overlapped boats; don't try to start at the starboard end of the line unless you approach on a close-hauled course. Otherwise you can be squeezed out.

After starting, things are easier because everyone is working upwind close-hauled, and either rule 36 or 37.1 will apply most of the time. As a port-tack boat, watch for starboard tackers (36). On either tack, watch for boats which may tack just ahead and below you; they gain rights as leeward or clear-ahead boats on the same tack (37.1 or 37.2). Before tacking into a position giving you right of way, be sure boats near you will have time to keep clear after you tack (41.2).

At the windward mark, plan to come in on starboard from

28 – The Yacht Racing Rules Today

at least four-to-five boat lengths away. If there is a boat to leeward overlapping you, give her room to round the mark even if it requires a luff on your part. Anyone on port tack must avoid you, however.

On the reaching legs, boats ahead and to leeward can force you to change course. If overlapped with a leeward boat, give her right of way.

Rounding the next mark, if overlapped, give or ask (loudly, ahead of time) for room, depending on whether you are outside or inside boat.

At the leeward mark the same rules apply but watch for outside boats rounding up sharply to their close-hauled courses after clearing the mark. Rule 37.1 gives them normal leeward-boat rights even though they may have had to give insiders room while rounding.

Finally, at the finish it is safest to approach on starboard tack. Remember to give room, at either end, to any insiders sailing on the same tack.

If your objective is to master just the fundamentals of the rules, you may want to concentrate exclusively on the basics and their related definitions. Most of the time they will serve you well enough. Even if you do plan to get acquainted with the other rules and definitions, you probably should spend more time with Chapter 2 of this book and your rulebook, unless of course you already have a solid knowledge of the fundamentals of Parts I and IV. If you want to build a firmer foundation, however, reread each of the basics, this time with some model boats or cardboard cutouts of boats that you can shift around on the living-room floor. Ask yourself how many different port-starboard encounters you can think of, for example, as you consider rule 36. Do the same for rule 37.1. Add a third boat and perhaps a fourth. In each case, decide which boats have right-of-way, and why. Then confirm your judgment with a look at the rulebook. This way, both the typical boat-to-boat encounters and the rules themselves will become more familiar to you. This moves you toward your objective of getting a near-instinctive knowledge of the basic rules.

Meanwhile—until you feel you know thoroughly all the rules of Part IV, race with these four principles in mind:

1. Avoid getting into messes; especially stay away from crowds of boats.
2. Don't change course abruptly when near others.
3. Don't hit anyone!
4. Assume the other skipper knows the rules better than you do. If in doubt, give way.

Beyond the basics, Part IV of the rulebook includes several other important rules. Chapters 3 and 4 cover these and some important frequently expressed principles. We will begin with them.

3

Beyond the Basics—Part I

Each of the few rules we looked at in Chapter 2 has its special fine points. In this chapter and the next we examine all the rules, in groups that bring closely related rules together. Keep your rulebook within reach. We will quote directly from it, but by looking at the rule in the book itself you will become accustomed to seeing it in a particular place. This can be helpful, especially when you are in a hurry to prepare for a protest hearing.

In referring to an important appeal, we will identify it this way: IYRU Case 23 is from the International Yacht Racing Union's "Interpretations of the Yacht Racing Rules 1963–72," NAYRU 67 is one of the North American Yacht Racing Union's "Decisions of the Appeals Committee," and RYA 67/7 is Case 7 of the 1967 Racing Appeals Cases of Britain's Royal Yachting Association.

Some Consistent Principles

The rules in Part IV reflect a few basic principles that are sometimes stated in different ways and sometimes stated only by implication. For example, we can infer from such words as "ample," "obvious," "clearly," and "presumably" that a jury or protest committee will give the benefit of the doubt to one party, in certain prescribed circumstances.

This same idea is stated formally in some rules, which say that the obligated boat has the "onus of satisfying the race committee" that she did not infringe the rule. This is a very mild form of the reverse of the familiar principle that one is presumed innocent until proven guilty. If there is an "onus" clause in a rule, and the facts as presented seem to leave the decision hanging in the balance, the protest committee should rely on the onus principle by giving the benefit of the doubt to the party the rule was designed to protect.

Sometimes the appeals themselves create a burden on an accused to prove himself innocent. Rule 36 neither states nor implies any onus, yet the port-tack boat must, according to the law found in the appeals, very nearly prove that she kept clear. In this sense, rule 36 is unique. Be aware, therefore, of those rules in which there is a degree of presumed guilt imposed on one party by the onus clause, by a certain word that implies it, or by the weight of the appeals.

The appeals also have something specific to say about the onus idea. RYA 63/17 discusses the weight that this clause ought to have; in it a port-tack boat tacked to leeward of a starboard-tack boat but was not found guilty of infringing rule 41.1 or 41.2. The race committee had felt that there was "reasonable doubt" as to whether the tacking boat had tacked too close aboard the other, and asked whether it was nevertheless bound to impose the penalty. The appeals committee said that if the "weight of the evidence tends to show" that the onus-bearing boat did *not* foul, then she should go unpenalized. The *stated* onus clause is thus not a major burden, and good committees will use it only as an "other things being equal" consideration. The idea that one is innocent until proven otherwise does obtain generally, except for the strange exception of rule 36.

A more clear-cut principle found in the rules is that hailing is desirable for purposes of safety and sportsmanship, and when there is any doubt, a hail should be made. There is never a penalty for hailing (unless it was deliberate deception, when rule 49 would apply), and there is often a reward. On the other hand there is sometimes a penalty for not hailing, but never a reward. Rules 35, 38.3, 43, 46.2, and indirectly, 41 and 42 all can involve hailing. Any rule defining right-of-way can be reinforced with a hail.

A third principle is that a boat not only need not anticipate acquiring an obligation to give way or keep clear, but also must be allowed reasonable time to respond after she does acquire the obligation. IYRU 53 (also NAYRU 140, discussed on page 109) is a dramatic illustration. Other appeals make the same point. Rule 37.3's and 44.1(b)'s "ample room and opportunity" phrase is an explicit statement of the idea, as is part of rule 40 and all of rule 42.2(a)(ii). Both rules 41.2 and 42.2(d)(i) say a right-of-way boat need not anticipate the loss of some of her rights. Rule 34, one of the most important in Part IV, establishes a very closely related principle: a right-of-way boat should not make it difficult for an obligated boat to meet her obligations. Watch how these general principles come into play in this chapter and the next.

Part IV of the rulebook is broken into six sections, A through F. Their headings are not rules themselves, but are one way to keep groups of rules straight. Sections A and E have particularly important headings. The rules in Section A are never overridden by rules in other sections (although rule 34 of Section A does have two important exceptions, which are rules of other sections). The rules of Section E sometimes (not always) are in conflict with a rule of Section B, C, or D, and when they are the Section E rules prevail.

Another fine point in the introductory note to Section E is that if a rule is in conflict with an earlier rule within Section E the later rule takes precedence. Thus Section E rules have priority over all rules of Sections B, C, and D, and earlier Section E rules. Remember, however, that Section E rules do not necessarily conflict with others and if they do not, the earlier rules still stand.

On Opposite Tacks

As already noted, the sole rule in Section B (opposite-tack rule) is 36, requiring port-tack boats to keep clear of starboard-tack boats. Although a clear-cut statement, this rule does not give absolute freedom to S. ("S" means a boat on starboard tack. See page x for other designations.)

Other rules sometimes restrict S's freedom of movement. Rule 42 is already a familiar example; if outside at marks or obstructions on offwind legs she must give room to Ps (port-tack boats) who are insiders. If inside a port-tacker when the next leg calls for a jibe, she must jibe (unless she has rule-38 luffing rights, discussed later). Also, in less-common circumstances, she must keep clear of boats in trouble—those capsized or aground—as well as boats merely anchored.

She can also lose her rights through error. After a premature start, or hitting a mark, while correcting her mistake she must keep clear of others not in the same predicament (rules 44 and 45).

34 – The Yacht Racing Rules Today

In still other circumstances S's rights are not cancelled, yet they are limited. Rule 34, already discussed in Chapter II, prevents her from interfering with boats trying to keep clear of her. She must not assert her rights without giving warning and thus cause a collision resulting in serious damage (rule 35.1). In coming to marks or obstructions without an overlap on a port-tack boat ahead, S must stay clear in anticipation of P's rounding (rule 42.1(b)(i)). She must not establish an overlap between a P and a continuing obstruction unless there is room to do so safely (rule 42.2 (c)).

Nonetheless, being on starboard tack generally has significant advantages. Maneuvering before the start, approaching windward marks, overtaking or sailing alongside others on a run, and approaching the finish line all call for being on starboard if the water is crowded. Note also the definitions "On a Tack" and "Leeward and Windward." You are on starboard tack if your boom is over your port side, because your tack corresponds to your windward side, which is the side opposite your boom. Thus a boat sailing by the lee may still be on starboard tack.

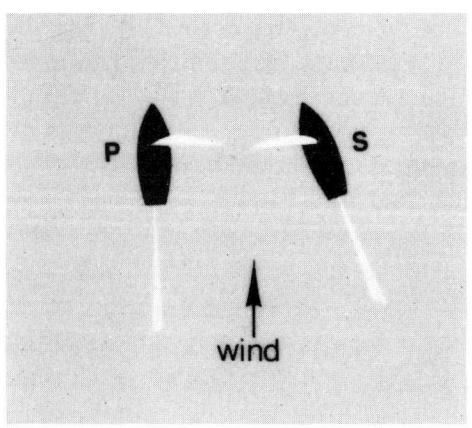

Boats without shrouds, such as the Finn, Sunfish, and Laser, can ease their booms well forward and are thereby able to steer well off the dead-run course.

As already mentioned, an interesting and very important fact in your understanding of rule 36 (and of the nature of the appeals) is that rule 36 does not explicitly put the onus on P of satisfying the race committee that she kept clear; yet the onus is there, and is definitely P's. Further, although the onus principle is rather mild in its application to other rules (the accused party need not *prove* his innocence, and the principle is an "if in doubt" one), when applied to rule-36 situations it is very strong indeed.

How can P be made to bear the onus when the rules say nothing about it? The answer is that several appeals consistently give the benefit of the doubt, regardless of how flimsy the doubt itself may be, to S. These appeals are illustrations of the fact, mentioned in Chapter 1, that the appeals sometimes make new law themselves. Perhaps rule 36 will someday be made to say what the appeals interpret it to mean; meanwhile, consider four important appeals.

In NAYRU 32, two 8-meters were converging, on a weather leg, and S bore off below P when twenty feet from her, and passed astern of her within about five feet. P was disqualified. The appeals committee said there was "reasonable doubt" whether P could have crossed S; S was therefore "entitled" to bear away. Further, it said the onus lay on P, and P failed to convince the committee that she would have crossed successfully.

In RYA 65/1, P had slightly overstood the weather mark and was close-reaching just above the port-tack lay line. S, approaching P, slowed down and later protested. She won her case because testimony from S, P, and various witnesses left the committee in doubt. The appeals committee's decision was that since the race committee had decided that the *possibility* of a collision existed, P was correctly disqualified. Their decision included a quotation from an 1876 decision that said that P should be disqualified "in all cases where the *slightest* risk of collision may be satisfactorily proved" (italics added). This is a much stronger prescription than the onus principle and probably would not be supported in North America or Britain today. Contrast it with RYA 65/9, in which rules 37 and 39 applied. As is true of rule 36, no onus is stipulated by either of these rules. Two boats were overlapped and W (windward) bore off on L (leeward), and L said later that she bore off to avoid W. The local race committee asked whether W bore any onus to convince them of her innocence. The appeals committee said no; L's bearing off was not sufficient evidence that W was guilty. In rule 36 the obligated boat is usually presumed guilty but in 37 she is not.

Our fourth case is more recent. NAYRU 137 discusses a finish-line incident, P trying to cross S. S tacked when P began to cross, and P was disqualified. Confirming the decision, the appeals committee commented that "the onus . . . is basically P's." It also said that race committees should be certain that there is some doubt, in such cases, that P would have cleared S.

As a practical matter, then, you take your chances when you try to cross ahead of a starboard-tack boat. If S bears off, or tacks instead, that fact will be given heavy weight by the protest committee. Moreover, they will expect you to convince them that there was, in fact, no doubt about your ability to cross S, and doing that will be difficult.

There is another important implication to be drawn from these appeals, and from the significance given to a starboard-tack boat's taking avoiding action. It helps give meaning to the phrase "keep clear." These words mean not only "do not touch" the other boat; they also mean "do not sail so close to the other boat that she will be frightened into taking avoiding action." In short, the possibility of a collision may exist only in the mind of the other skipper, but the rules recognize it as a real hazard just the same.

Rules 41.1–4 are the whole of Section D, "Changing Tack Rules." They can apply when a leeward boat of two Ps decides to become an S:

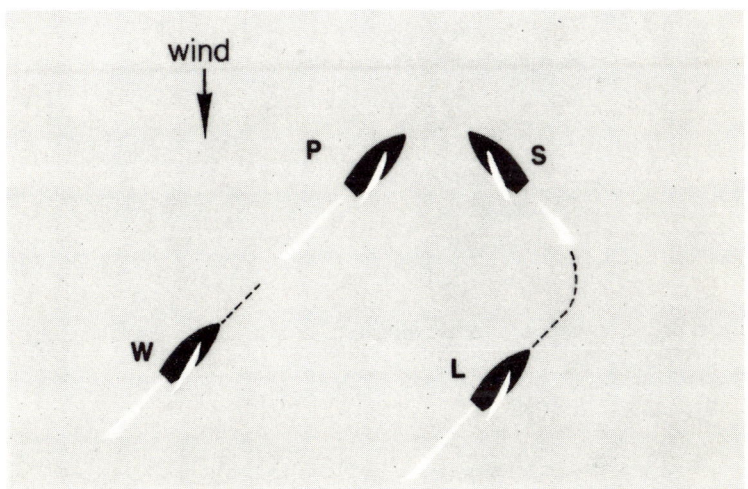

a P decides to become an LS:

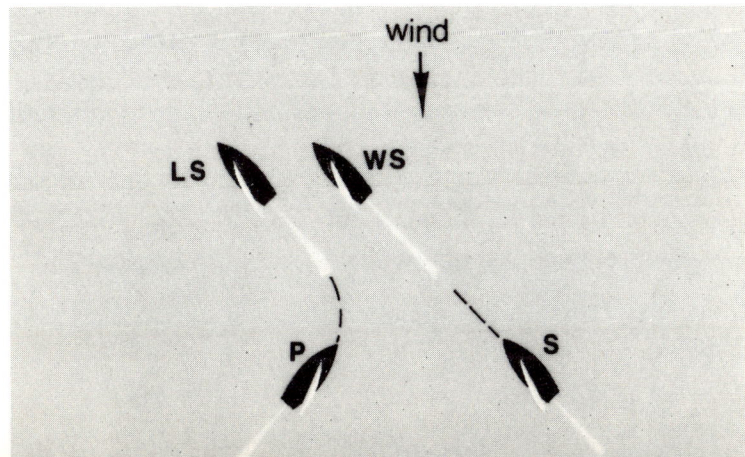

38 — The Yacht Racing Rules Today

when on a run a windward boat decides to become an S:

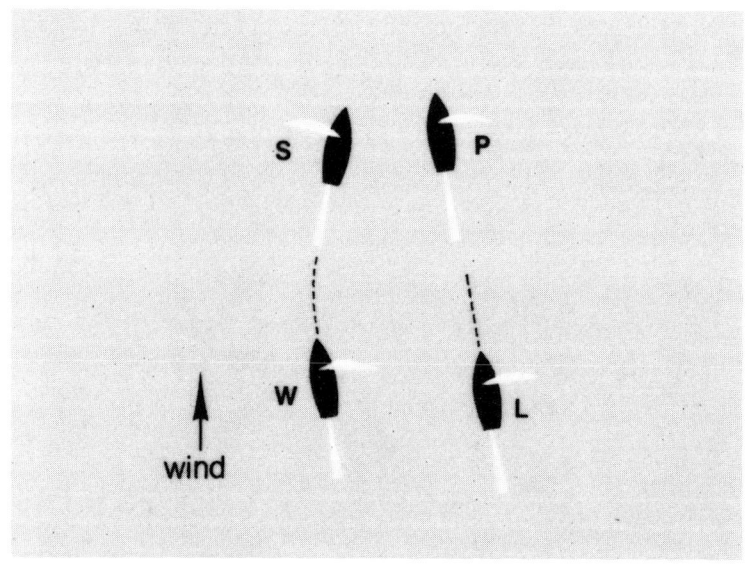

and often before the start as boats jockey back and forth behind the line.

Rule 41.1 says this:

A yacht which is either **tacking** or **jibing** shall keep clear of a yacht **on a tack.**

Read the definitions of tacking and jibing, especially tacking. Tacking does not begin until a boat has passed the head-to-wind stage of her maneuver. During the first half of her swing through the wind she is only luffing. The rules recognize only the second half as tacking. Still, a few seconds do elapse while the tack takes place.

Jibing is different. It begins and ends in virtually the same instant of time. The mainsail fills when there is wind in it, and the wind must be in it in order for the boom to be blown across the hull. In any case, even if it is argued that "filled" means the boom being in normal sailing position after the jibe, the passage of time is extremely brief.

Note also that with modern jibing techniques the change in a boat's course has occurred before the jibe. Good procedure for most boats calls for steering away from the windward side to encourage the boom to cross, then bearing off sharply as it does:

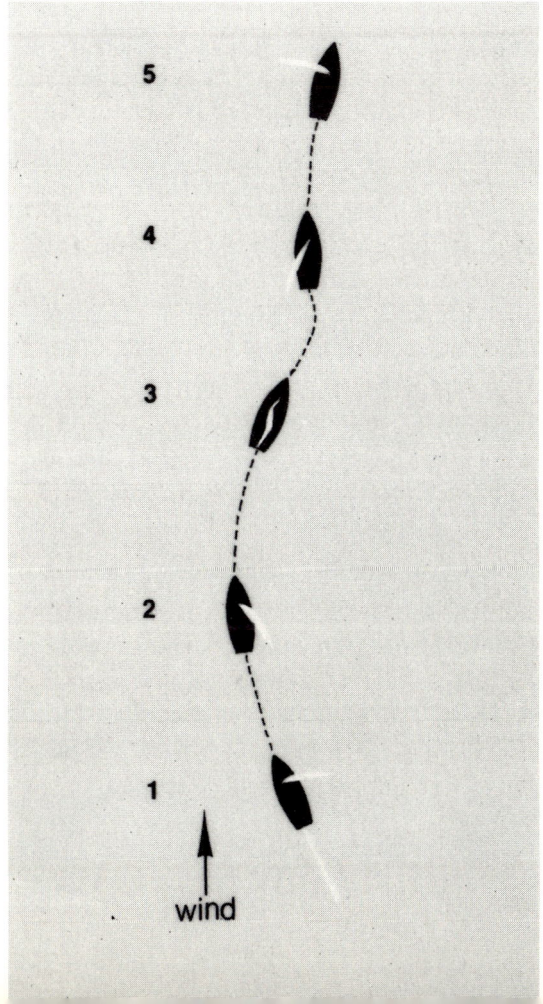

The jibe takes place between stages 3 and 4. The stern has already passed through the wind; the definition's phrase "with the wind aft" is only a general reference to wind direction in relation to the boat's course, included to distinguish the jibing definition from the tacking definition.

Rule 41.1 merely says "keep clear" while you are tacking or jibing. Heeding the rule is usually easy because the tacking and jibing processes are so short.

It is rule 41.2 that bears down more heavily on a boat that changes tacks:

> A yacht shall neither **tack** nor **jibe** into a position which will give her right of way unless she does so far enough from a yacht **on a tack** to enable this yacht to keep clear without having to begin to alter her course until after the **tack** or **jibe** has been completed.

In fewer words, a boat that will become obligated to keep clear as the result of another's tack or jibe need not anticipate her obligation. Incidentally, this is one of the explicit statements of the principle that an about-to-be obligated boat need not anticipate her new obligation.

Rule 41.2 gets added punch from 41.3, one of the explicit provisions of the onus requirement:

> A yacht which **tacks** or **jibes** has the onus of satisfying the race committee that she completed her **tack** or **jibe** in accordance with rule 41.2.

On windward legs, tactics or strategy often call for a change of tack that will give the tacking boat right-of-way afterward. Review the diagrams on page 37. Rules 41.1–3 protect the other boat from a too-sudden confrontation. However, especially when a port tacker tacks into a safe leeward position, they also give the tacking boat an advantage.

The key to this advantage lies in the definition of tacking, where it says that a boat's tack is complete when she has "borne away, if beating to windward, *to a close-hauled course*" (italics added). Her speed, the position of her sails, and the heel of her hull are all quite irrelevant. It is getting to the close-hauled course that determines the moment when she gains rights as a leeward or clear-ahead boat under rules 37.1 or 37.2.

IYRU 32 makes this crystal clear:

When beating to windward, a yacht has completed her tack when she is heading on a close-hauled course regardless of her movement through the water or the sheeting of her sails.

Committees generally have become aware of the tacking boat's rights in such cases, although doubtless there will be some who tend to think that the nontacking boat has virtue completely on her side. NAYRU 50 was a correction of such a decision. In it, P had tacked in front of S, and S had then tacked away, about three seconds after P was on course. S's protest under rule 41.2 was sustained by the local committee. The appeals committee reversed the decision, reasoning that the fact that S had had time to tack after P had gained a close-hauled course showed that P had not tacked too close.

Don't forget that rule 41.2 and the definition of jibing also combine to define a jibing boat's obligations and rights on leeward legs. Although the course change is less (usually only 20–30 degrees compared with the 90 or so normally required for tacking), and therefore the likelihood of fouling is less, the jibing boat still must keep clear while jibing, and the other boat still must begin to keep clear as soon as (but not before) the jiber's sail "has filled."

We will see two exceptions to rules 41.1 and 41.2 when we come to rule 42. Before or during a mark-rounding, for example, the boat inside or ahead is entitled to make her jibe without interference from a boat outside or behind (rules 42.1(a)(i) and 42.1(b)(i)).

On the Same Tack—Preliminaries

Once two boats are overlapped on the same tack their rights and obligations are defined by basic rule 37.1, plus two forms of a rather odd provision for allowing a leeward boat to attack another by luffing (rules 38 and 40), and a special offwind rule (39) that limits the windward boat's actions. Before looking at these groups of rules we need first to consider two rules that apply just before a leeward boat gains her 37.1 rights.

One of these we saw in Chapter 2's third basic, expressed in rule 37.2:

> A yacht **clear astern** shall keep clear of a yacht **clear ahead.**

Let your imagination conjure up what can happen just before a start, and rule 37.2 becomes quite interesting. When a group of boats are stalling side by side on the line with little space between, a boat behind them (see diagram on page 18) has no right to expect them to move ahead. They may not be moving and it is even possible to imagine one of them moving backward. Booms may be out, sails luffing. To solve this "second tier" problem you need to avoid it earlier by getting a place in the first tier.

By approaching the boat ahead from one side or the other you avoid problems with rule 37.2, and if you choose the leeward side you benefit from 37.1 after the overlap begins.

Beyond the Basics—Part I – 43

However, you first must avoid a hazard created by rule 37.3, which says in part:

> A yacht which establishes an **overlap** to **leeward** from **clear astern** shall allow the **windward** yacht ample room and opportunity to keep clear . . .

This is protection for W against L coming in so close or so fast that W has neither the time nor space to respond. Here we meet again the principle that anticipation is not required of a boat that is about to become obligated. The key phrase is *"ample* room and opportunity." "Opportunity" implies both time and space and could stand alone, but adding "room" makes it doubly clear that W is entitled both to enough time so that she need not begin keeping clear before the overlap begins, and to enough space to do it in. Since boats pivot around their centerboards or keels, a W that wants to steer away from L will be able to move her bow to windward only by swinging her stern to leeward:

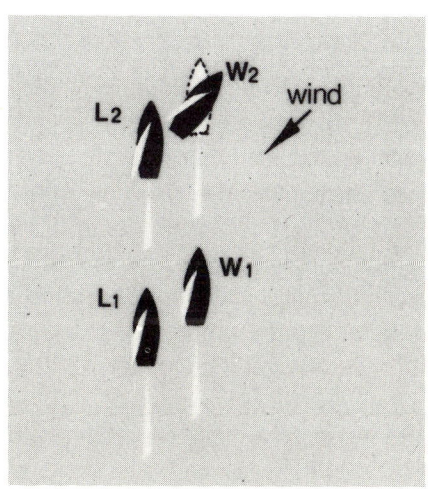

This explains the need for rule 37.3; if boats pivoted at their sterns as do automobiles, the rule might never have been invented.

The word "ample" is extremely powerful, because it is an onus word. It puts the onus on L, because it means "plenty," "quite enough," or "more than enough." Check your own dictionary. It decidedly means more room than merely "just sufficient." Protest committees will give any benefit of the doubt to W.

How much time and how much space are required? As for time, L's obligation is short-lived. If W does not complain just as soon as the overlap begins, or begin taking her avoiding action immediately, she is in trouble. In NAYRU 36, L overtook W before the start and W did not keep clear. W was disqualified. The appeals committee said that L's obligation under rule 37.3 "cannot be construed as a continuing one." W failed to take "prompt and decisive" measures to keep clear. IYRU 46 confirms this principle. Therefore, when in W's position, be sure to *begin* to take avoiding action right away.

On the other hand, the rule does not require that you *complete* your avoiding action immediately; you are allowed reasonable time to do this. In NAYRU 126, W was "nearly wayless" when L overlapped her. As we have seen, W was not obligated to anticipate the overlap, and waylessness is not a rule violation. W did begin to trim her sails when the overlap began, and she was upheld by the appeals committee.

Time is one thing but space is another, and once again we find the appeals not only illuminating the rules, but also adding substance to them. The result is that W can alter course as much as she pleases, short of actually tacking. She can luff all the way to a head-to-wind position. If in the process she hits L with her stern, L will lose the protest, because the contact will be considered evidence that L did not allow ample room. IYRU 46 confirms this, in replying to a series of questions about an L that established her overlap to leeward of W's stern but not to leeward of her boom, while both were reaching:

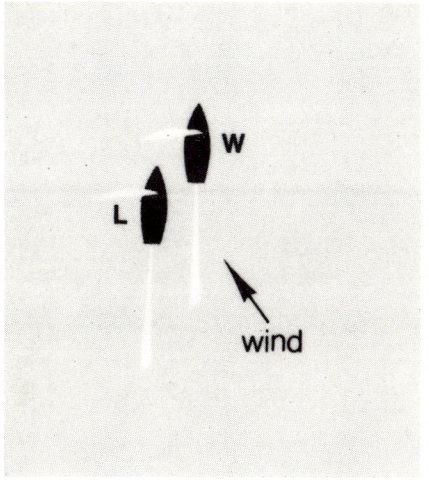

The essence of L's compliance with rule 37.3's "room" requirement has nothing to do with whether L's course takes her inside W's boom, but depends solely on whether W had room to luff *head-to-wind*.

To sum up, when an overlap from clear astern begins, if you are W, begin your course change and/or sail trim as soon as the overlap begins. You may luff fast, and as high as you wish. You need not anticipate your obligation, and may take the necessary time to steer away or trim sails. If you are L, leave enough room for W's stern to swing toward you if she luffs all the way. If she does not begin to respond when the overlap begins, she has no defense under rule 37.3, and rule 37.1 applies immediately thereafter.

On the Same Tack, Overlapped

This brings us to a group of rules that control boat-to-boat relationships once an overlap has been established and the time for applying the first part of rule 37.3 has come and gone. These include the second half of rule 37.3, rule 39, and of course the basic rule—37.1. The special luffing rules (38 and 40) also apply; we will examine them separately. For now, assume that the leeward boat does not have these luffing rights.

With regard to rule 37.3, its second part states:

. . . during the existence of that **overlap** the **leeward yacht** shall not sail above her **proper course.**

The definition of a proper course is that it is

. . . any course which a yacht might sail after the starting signal, in the absence of the other yacht or yachts affected, to **finish** as quickly as possible. The course sailed before **luffing** or **bearing away** is *presumably*, but not necessarily, that yacht's **proper course**. There is no **proper course** before the starting signal. (Italics added.)

The meaning of "proper course" is worth studying. It is not necessarily a course of constant direction. In most boats, one should sail a reach, for example, by bearing off in the gusts and heading up in the lulls. "Presumably" in the definition, at first glance, appears to be an onus word that would throw the benefit of the doubt against a boat that luffed during an overlap, but that had not sailed such a course before. Yet the appeals show that you are entitled to make your own judgment of your proper course, within broad bounds of reasonableness. NAYRU 6 states, "When there is doubt that a yacht is sailing above her proper course, she should be given the benefit of the doubt." IYRU 25 says that the test of a proper course is whether a boat has a "logical" reason for it and applies this reason with "some" consistency.

It is not hard to understand why you might be confused between our initial assumption that L does not have "luffing rights," on the one hand, and on the other, what we have just learned about a leeward boat having the right to luff as long as she is sailing a proper course. The answer is that "luffing rights" is a misleading phrase when applied to the special luffing rights given by rules 38 and 40. The right to luff is not defined exclusively by those rules, as we will see shortly. Meanwhile, be clear in your own mind that although rule 37.3 prohibits L from sailing above her proper course, it does not prohibit her from luffing *per se*. Even more surprising, rule 37.1 in combination with the "proper course" definition allows L to luff without first obtaining the "mast abeam" position, which is a condition of the special luffing rights described in rules 38 and 40.

Several appeals reveal this. In IYRU 11, L overtook W on a broad reach, moved abeam, then luffed slightly and touched W. W lost the case; she had failed to keep clear as required by rule 37.1. L was not guilty of sailing above her proper course; she said she had luffed in order to head more directly toward the next mark.

In IYRU 25, L and W were reaching on the starboard tack. To windward was an area of lighter wind, but the current they were fighting was also weaker. To leeward, the wind was stronger but so was the current. L, without rule 38.1's luffing rights, decided to go inshore for the weaker current and luffed in order to do so. W did not get out of the way and the two made contact. The appeals committee said that W had violated rule 37.1, but that L had not violated rule 37.3. Whether her judgment about the benefits of going inshore was valid was immaterial; what mattered was that her reason for doing so was plausible.

In a windward leg situation described in NAYRU 6, L and W approached the mark to be left to port, overlapped on the starboard tack. They were slightly high of the lay line. When about five lengths from it, W bore off and they touched. W lost the case; the appeals committee said that L could not be held guilty of sailing above her proper course, because her course, if held, would have taken her the wrong side of the mark by less than a length. This is the case mentioned earlier where L's being entitled to the benefit of the doubt was stated.

Rule 39 places limitations on all windward boats or boats clear ahead, before or during overlap encounters:

> A yacht which is on a free leg of the course shall not sail below her **proper course** when she is clearly within three of her overall lengths of either a **leeward yacht** or a yacht **clear astern** which is steering a course to pass to **leeward.**

Just as a windward leg is one on which a boat must tack at least once in order to reach the end of the leg, a free leg is any leg that can be sailed without tacking. Most of us think immediately of standard reaches and runs, but rule 39 also applies on a very close-winded leg. On windward legs, the fact that it does not apply means that a windward boat is not prohibited from sailing below her proper course to hinder a leeward boat. But remember: the leeward boat still has rule 37.1 to lean on, so the windward boat must not force her to alter course.

Note the loophole in rule 39. It is not a prohibition against bearing off in front of a boat that is behind, if that boat is not "steering a course to pass to leeward." She may be right behind you, but if her course would take her directly to you, or to windward of you, you are free to sail below your proper course. The rule would apply here:

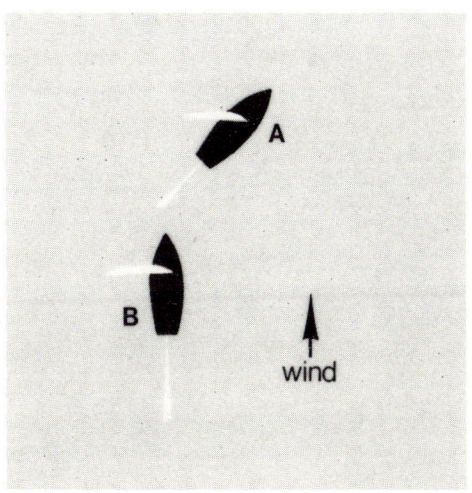

or here:

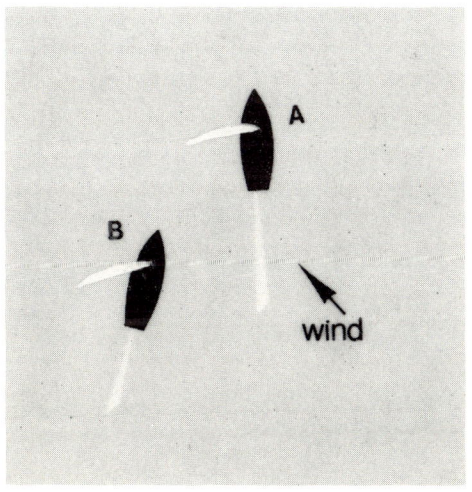

but not here:

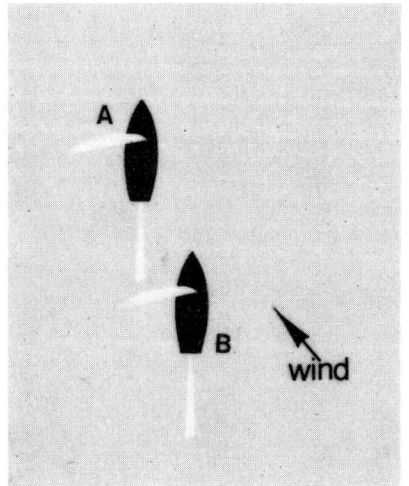

or here:

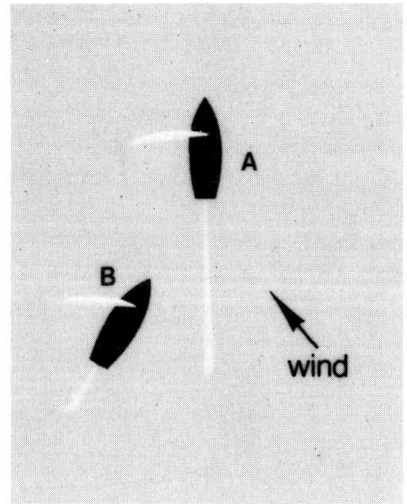

Beyond the Basics—Part I – 51

Note also that the rule does not prohibit bearing off. It says only that the boat ahead or to windward may not sail below her proper course. She is free to bear off in the gusts, for example, or because she wants to get to an area of slack current. As long as she is not overlapped with a boat overtaking her, she is free to bear off as much as she can justify within the concept of proper course. Once they are overlapped, rule 37.1 restricts her freedom of movement but she can nevertheless move quite close to L.

The definition of proper course gives an interesting twist to rule 39. In the diagram, B is trying to pass A to leeward and must bear off to do so:

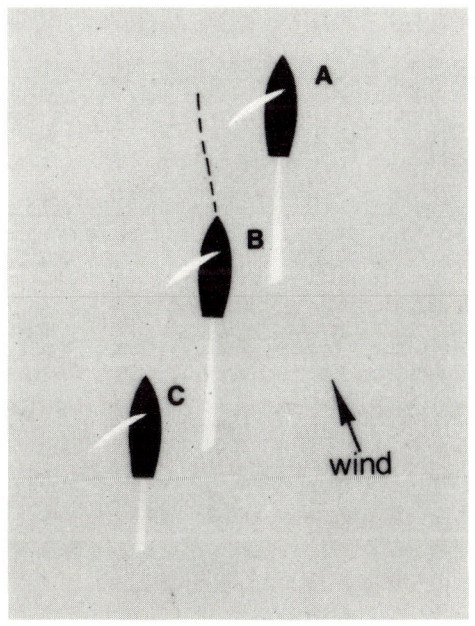

In the absence of A, she would be infringing rule 39 by bearing off within three lengths of C. But the definition of proper course says it is a course "a yacht might sail . . . *in the absence of the other yacht or yachts affected*, to finish as quickly as possible" (italics added). The boat "affected" by B's course change is C. In the absence of C, B would bear off to pass A. Thus B is not sailing below her proper course when she bears off. To be sure, she cannot interfere with C (rule 37.1 is C's protection) but B need not worry about rule 39.

There is a mild onus word in rule 39; it is "clearly." If there is doubt as to whether the boats were within three lengths of one another, and the boat ahead or to windward bore off, the benefit of the doubt is in her favor. All in all, rule 39 is not a very strong rule, in view of what we know about "proper course" generally being interpreted in favor of the boat whose course is in question. Nevertheless, its intent is fairness; the boat ahead or to windward is considered to have the advantage, and therefore she should be discouraged from going out of her way to make trouble for a boat behind or to leeward which is trying to pass to leeward.

Now we can put together rules 37.1–3, 39, and the "proper course" idea. As a group, they relate closely to one another. Let's consider two boats, reaching on starboard tack. One comes from astern, establishes an overlap to leeward of the other, and they sail together that way for some time.

Taking our rules in sequence, 37.2 requires the boat astern to keep clear. At the same time, 39 requires the boat ahead to sail no lower than her proper course, if the other boat is steering a course that will take her to leeward of the boat ahead. Next, at the moment the overlap begins, 37.3 obligates the leeward boat to allow time and space for the windward boat to take avoiding action. At the same time and after, W is bound by 37.1 to keep clear of L, and she remains bound by 39 not to sail below her proper course. L is bound by 37.3 not to sail above *her* proper course.

Of the four rules, three of them create continuing obligations; 37.1 and 39 apply to W, and 37.3 to L. Since 37.3 and 39 deal with "proper course," that definition can be critically important. The nub of it is that both L and W may have different proper courses, and if the two courses would bring the boats together it is basic rule 37.1 that applies. Watch it in action, in two interesting protests.

In NAYRU 74, L overtook W and gradually luffed until the two touched. W lost the case because she had not kept clear under rule 37.1, and because L had not sailed above her proper course. In NAYRU 127, two starboard tackers on a broad reach approached a mark, their courses taking them closer and closer to each other. L was forced to bear off to avoid W. W had not sailed below her proper course, but neither had L sailed above hers. Rule 37.1 gave L the case.

A final word on rule 37.1; usually it applies in rather slow-moving situations, the boats involved sailing in approximately the same direction. However, as we saw in Chapter 2, it can also apply between boats beating up to a windward mark and those that have just rounded:

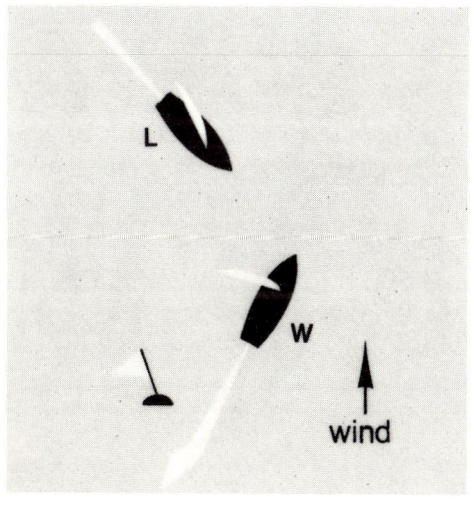

If you are W, be cautious about sailing close to L. A wind shift may change her course and, as a result, your calculations. Rude 34 prohibits her from obstructing you, but because the two boats are closing on one another so rapidly your freedom of movement is already severely limited. Rule 34 probably will not help you much in a protest hearing.

Special Luffing Rights

Rules 38 and 40, entitled "Right-of-Way Yacht Luffing After Starting" and "Before Starting," respectively, do not say all there is to be said about luffing rights, as our discussion of rule 37 attempted to show. Rule 38, especially, might be better labeled "Special Luffing Rights," because it allows a boat already holding right-of-way under rule 37.1 to luff suddenly and without warning. It is thus the major exception to our fifth basic (see page 23). It is listed twice as an exception to the rules of Section A, "Rules Which Always Apply." The first is in rule 34. Thus rule 38's special luffing rights allow a boat to alter course to try to obstruct or prevent another boat from keeping clear. The second is in rule 35; there, a hail is not only not required, but if a damaging collision occurs the luffing boat will be held guiltless.

In short, rule 38 sanctions an outright attack on one boat by another, virtually disregarding safety considerations. The fact that it is not used much may be explained by sailors' feelings that it is a form of dirty playing or that going out of one's way to engage in a luffing match can be very expensive in time lost to the rest of the fleet. In any event, rule 38 is an interesting one with some colorful case history:

Luffing Rights and Limitations. After she has **started** and cleared the starting line, a yacht **clear ahead** or a **leeward yacht** may **luff** as she pleases, except that:—

> A **leeward yacht** shall not sail above her **proper course** while an **overlap** exists if, at any time during its existence, the helmsman of the **windward yacht** (when sighting abeam from his normal station and sailing no higher than the leeward yacht) has been abreast or forward of the mainmast of the **leeward yacht.**

As a rule of Section C ("Same Tack Rules"), 38.1 applies only to boats on the same tack. It applies just as rule 40 ceases to apply: when the luffing boat has cleared the starting line. The phrase "as she pleases" well expresses the luffing boat's freedom to turn just as sharply or suddenly as she wishes. She can luff head-to-wind, and retains her rights under rules 37.1 or 37.2 because she is still on the same tack. (Re-read the definitions of Luffing, On a Tack, and Tacking.)

It is the second part of rule 38.1 that describes the test for whether or not the rule's special luffing rights are available. When they are not, L may not sail above her proper course. Note that in this regard, the second part of rule 37.3 and the second part of 38.1 say exactly the same thing.

To understand the "mast abeam" test, keep in mind that it has two aspects: one is the physical positions of the two boats, and the other is the timing of events.

The physical test is whether a line projected abeam through the skipper's station will intersect the leeward boat at or forward of its mast, subject to one condition: the windward boat's course may be no higher than that of the leeward boat. This condition is needed, because as W pivots to a higher course, her skipper's sight line swings forward. Here are two examples showing leeward boats whose positions meet the physical test for special luffing rights; they are only just forward of "mast abeam":

56 — The Yacht Racing Rules Today

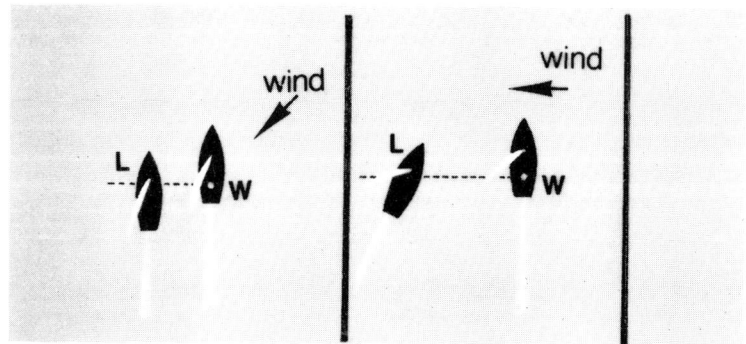

This physical test has some interesting properties, because the initial distance between the boats determines how quickly the windward boat gains "mast abeam" when both luff together. If they are close to begin with, a 20-degree course change will not eliminate L's special luffing rights unless she was only just able to claim them:

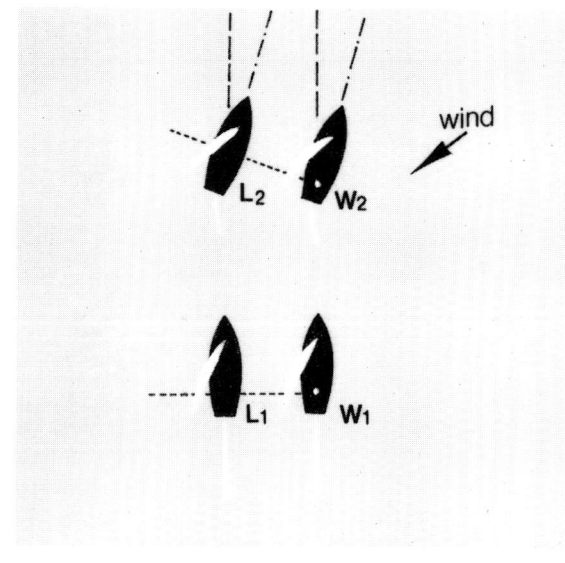

The same degree of course change would allow W to break L's hold on her, however, if they had been farther apart laterally when the luff began:

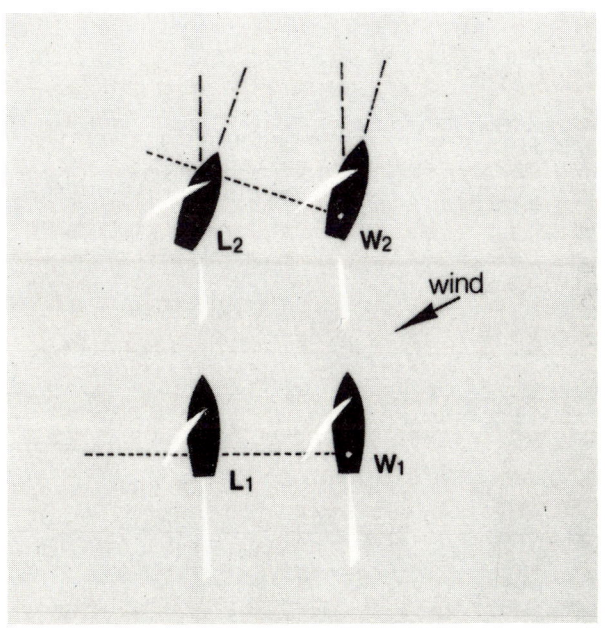

The second part of the test is chronological: was W's helmsman at *any* time forward of the "mast abeam" position during this overlap? If so, L has no special luffing rights. In all the illustrations above the "mast abeam" position itself would be insufficient if W had gained the "mast abeam" position previously, even though she subsequently lost it.

Because L's luffing rights under rule 38.1 depend on whether W had gained "mast abeam" at any time during a particular overlap, the different ways an overlap can begin and end become important. L may have overtaken W, in which case L would earn no special luffing rights, because W was forward of "mast abeam" right from the beginning. Or, W could overtake L. Then L would have her special luffing rights until W gained "mast abeam" or the overlap ended for some reason.

Rule 38.2 suggests four ways in which an overlap can begin or end, for purposes of rule 38.1. It is really a special definition rather than a right-of-way rule:

> **Overlap Limitations.** For the purpose of this rule: An **overlap** does not exist until the yachts are clearly within two overall lengths of the longer yacht; and an **overlap** which exists between two yachts when the leading yacht **starts**, or when one or both of them completes a **tack** or **jibe**, shall be regarded as a new **overlap** beginning at that time.

Reaching the starting line is one way, and if L had been aft of "mast abeam" during her prestart overlap with W, but had worked forward of it before hitting the line, she would be entitled to 38.1 luffing rights as soon as she cleared the line:

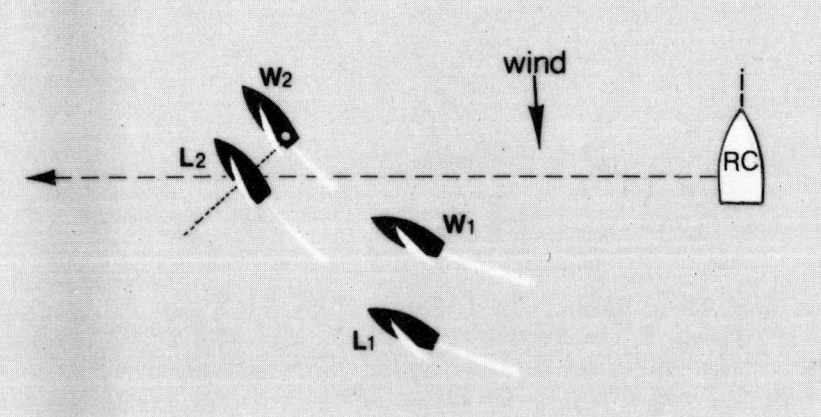

Or, L may gain her rights by tacking into them:

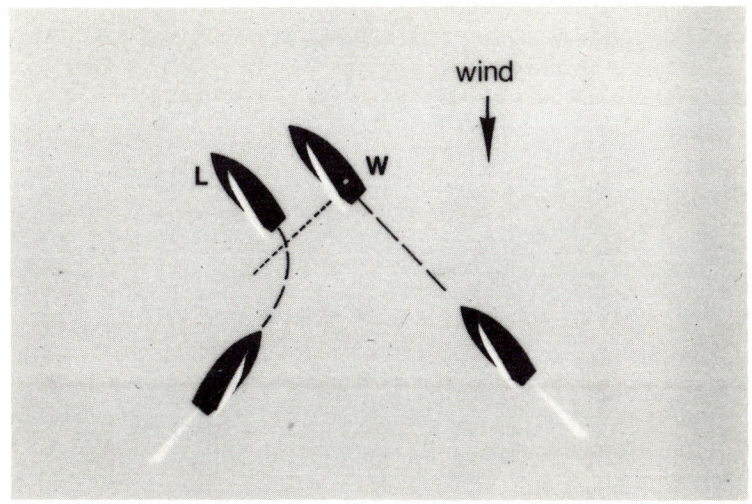

or jibing into them:

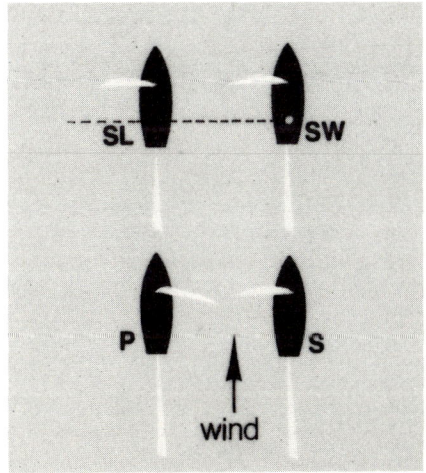

She may gain them by jibing twice, if she had overtaken W to leeward:

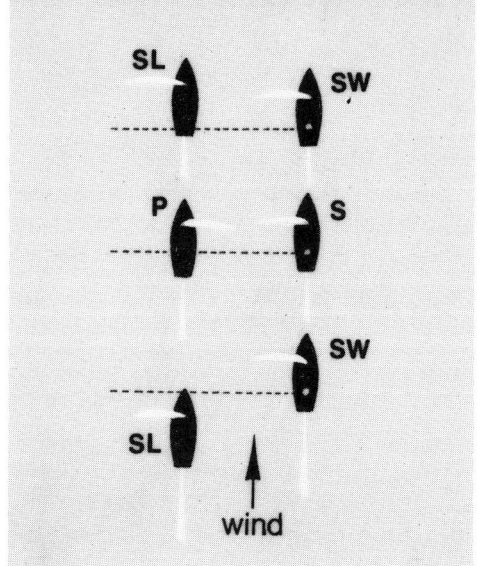

Also, she may gain them by widening out from W beyond the two-length limit:

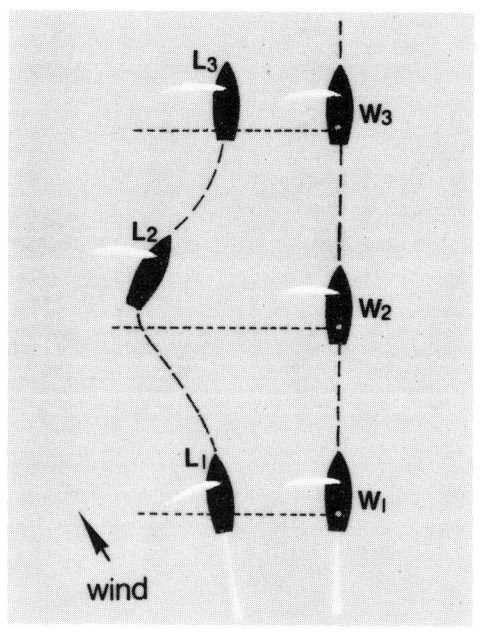

or simply by approaching from beyond the two-length limit:

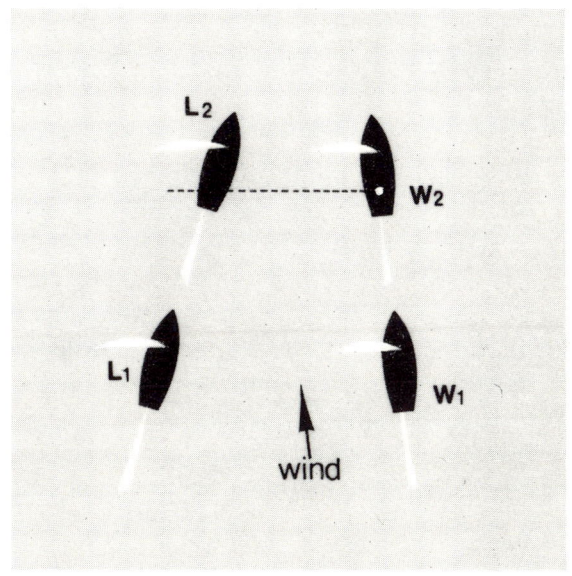

Notice the "onus" word: the overlap does not exist unless the boats are *clearly* within two lengths of each other. This can make it difficult for W to object to L's luff when, for example, L has overtaken W from astern, then widened out to leeward, then closed in again. L can argue that she gained a new overlap; the word "clearly" gives her a firm footing.

However, W also has a very strong weapon, given to her by rule 38.3:

Hailing to Stop or Prevent a Luff. When there is doubt, the **leeward yacht** may assume that she has the right to **luff** unless the helmsman of the **windward yacht** has hailed "Mast Abeam," or words to that effect. The **leeward yacht** shall be governed by such hail, and, if she deems it improper, her only remedy is to protest.

This rule gives W the authority to dictate L's rights, by allowing W to make the hail and requiring L to be bound by it. Looked at in another way, it also gives L the right to luff "when there is doubt" about the "mast abeam" test, and if W has not hailed her. If W is alert she will hail "Mast abeam" at the earliest permissible moment. If L feels that W hailed too early she must not only protest but argue convincingly that the facts justified her complaint. That is difficult to do.

Note that the "when there is doubt" phrase limits L's permission to luff any time W has not hailed. For example, as illustrated in NAYRU 78, when L has overtaken W close aboard there can be no doubt that W had "mast abeam" right from the start of the overlap. But any other time W should be sure to hail.

Once W has hailed "Mast abeam" she should not mistakenly assume that, because L must now fall off to her proper course, W is entitled to bear off immediately. L is still leeward boat, after all, and 37.1 is still on her side. In RYA 63/1, L luffed W and W hailed "Mast abeam." The local race committee asked whether W was permitted to bear off immediately. The appeals committee replied no, because L is the right-of-way boat under rule 37.1, and although she is obligated to "immediately assume" her proper course, W must allow her time to do so. This is yet another illustration of the "time for response" principle.

In another case (NAYRU 151), W hailed L but L continued to luff for another eight–ten seconds, and hit W. L was disqualified for failing to be governed by W's hail in rule 38.3. The appeals committee noted that it was a good thing that W had not borne off; otherwise she would have been in violation of rule 37.1.

Rule 38.4 at first seems to be somewhat superfluous, but it is not:

Beyond the Basics—Part I – 63

Curtailing a Luff. The **windward yacht** shall not cause a **luff** to be curtailed because of her proximity to the **leeward yacht** unless an **obstruction**, a third yacht or other object restricts her ability to respond.

This might seem to be translatable as "W may not violate L's luffing rights under rule 38.1," but it says more than that. It actually is a warning to W that she must anticipate the possibility that, as the two boats swing, she will be too close to L toward the end of the swing for L to be able to luff completely head-to-wind. If that happens, it proves that W did not respond in time, or was simply too close to L to begin with. And this is strictly W's problem, under rule 38.4. The rule does not say that W must anticipate L's obtaining luffing rights under 38.1, merely that she must anticipate that the space between the boats will quickly disappear as they pivot:

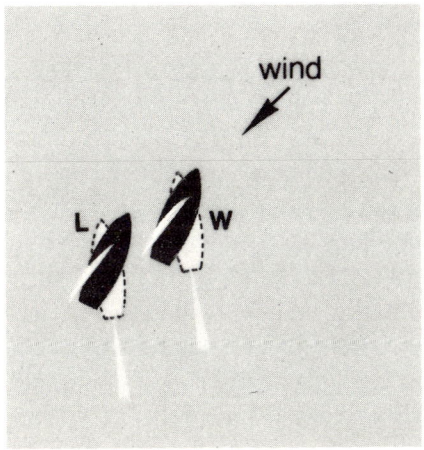

The exception is when W is prevented from responding by something else. Since the rule includes not only obstructions as legally defined, but also "third yachts" and "other objects,"

anything at all that keeps W from luffing will qualify. The third boat may or may not be subject to luffing under rule 38.1; if she is, but fails to respond, rule 38.4 protects the boat in the middle. Third boats may also hold right-of-way as opposite-tack boats; in any event they are obstructions. "Other objects" can also include a piling, too narrow to qualify as an obstruction under the definition of obstruction. Yet it would protect W from a collision with L.

Consideration of third boats brings us to rule 38.5:

Luffing Two or More Yachts. A yacht shall not **luff** unless she has the right to **luff** all yachts which would be affected by the **luff**, in which case they shall all respond even if an intervening yacht or yachts would not otherwise have the right to **luff**.

Thus, in a group of boats, the leewardmost of them must have been forward of "mast abeam" on all boats to windward of her. The windwardmost boat is entitled to hail "Mast abeam" to any leeward boat, and her hail restricts not only the hailed boat but anyone to leeward of that boat. If you are a boat between, you may be required to respond to a luff and, in the process, be luffing a boat to windward of you over whom you have no 38.1 rights; yet because of rule 38.5 the boats to windward of you must respond to your luff. You also may be extremely vulnerable. Because of the pivoting relationship we have already noted, a leeward boat that is aft of "mast abeam" will hit the boat to windward of her much sooner than if the leeward boat were forward of "mast abeam."

Two interesting appeals give additional substance to rule 38. In IYRU 3, L luffed, then bore away "hard" and hit W with her tiller extension. W lost the case, and the appeals committee said that L was entitled to bear away "both suddenly and rapidly." NAYRU 20 is similar, except that L hit W with her stern. The appeals committee made much the

Beyond the Basics—Part I – 65

same comments, noting that since rule 38 is an exception to rule 34, which forbids obstructing a boat which is keeping clear, L is not bound by 34.

The problem with the latter interpretation is that while 38.1 permits L to *luff* as she pleases, it does not give her blanket permission to use any other course change—i.e., bearing away—in disregard of rule 34. Nevertheless, be forewarned. Rule 38.1 is not only a powerful weapon for L as written but is even more powerful as interpreted.

When discussing rule 39 we saw that the definition of "proper course," referring to other "yachts affected," can add an interesting twist to a rule. It does this with rule 38 also. In the diagram, L has previously lost her 38.1 luffing rights, but wants to luff and attempt to pass A to windward. The "yacht affected" is W, and in her absence L would luff. She can do so here, therefore, because her proper course takes her to windward of A:

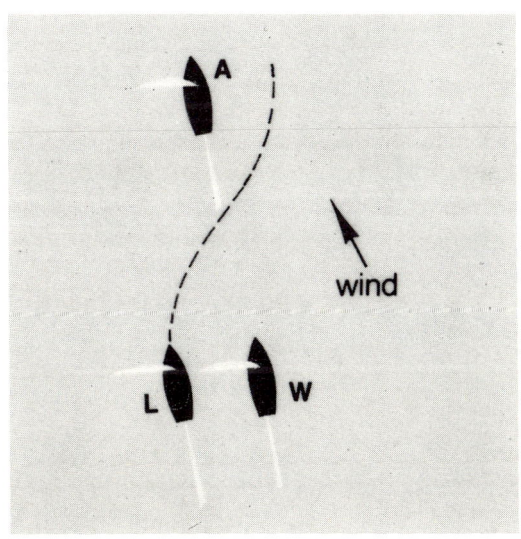

Rule 40, covering luffing before starting, is not so much a rule giving L special luffing rights before starting as it is a rule that allows her to exercise normal 37.1 rights before the "proper course" concept becomes operational. At the same time it offers considerable protection to W:

> Before a yacht has **started** and cleared the starting line, any **luff** on her part which causes another yacht to have to alter course to avoid a collision shall be carried out slowly and in such a way as to give the **windward yacht** room and opportunity to keep clear, but the **leeward yacht** shall not so **luff** above a **closed-hauled** course, unless the helmsman of the **windward yacht** (when sighting abeam from his normal station) is abaft the mainmast of the **leeward yacht**. Rules 38.3, Hailing to Stop or Prevent a Luff; 38.4, Curtailing a Luff; and 38.5, Luffing Two or More Yachts, also apply.

The differences between rules 40 and 38.1 make 40 much less of a threat to W with one exception: L is allowed to luff without gaining "mast abeam" at all. However, she may not luff above a close-hauled course until she has moved ahead of "mast abeam." Otherwise, W is less vulnerable under rule 40. After starting, L's luff can be sudden. Before, it must be done "slowly," an undefined word but one that probably would be intepreted in W's favor. After the start, L need not concern herself with giving W "room and opportunity." (This is the phrase we met in rule 37.3 but now "ample" has been left out.) Before the start, this phrase protects W by requiring L to give her a chance to keep clear even *after* the overlap begins. Rule 42.3 contains an exception to L's being allowed to luff head-to-wind if she is forward of "mast abeam" and we will cover that later.

Rules 38.3–5 also apply before starting. If W hails "Mast abeam," L must not luff above close-hauled, although she may luff up to close-hauled, as we have seen. To be allowed to luff more than one boat, L must have the same rights with respect to every boat to windward. If one of them has gained "mast abeam" then the close-hauled course limit applies.

Another extra protection to W is that the phrase "and sailing no higher than the leeward yacht" of rule 38.1 does not appear in rule 40. This means that W can luff higher than L's course and hail "Mast abeam," thereby limiting L's luff to a close-hauled course.

In summary, prestart luffing lets L sail a higher course as soon as she gains a leeward overlap on W. For this reason, while you are W, be sure to keep a sharp lookout for boats about to overlap you. As an L, if you want to luff, you will do well to hail loudly to W as soon as you have your overlap, and if W does not respond, continue hailing as you luff. Your luff must be done slowly, but it may be done steadily as soon as you have given W time and space to respond.

4

Beyond the Basics—Part II

Some of the more complicated rules are those in Section E, "Rules of Exception and Special Application." We will move in easy stages, first considering leeward marks. Bear in mind as we begin with rule 42.1(a)(i) that it also applies to obstructions, including other boats. We will add these complications later.

At Marks—Off the Wind

Our fourth basic rule said, "When overlapped with inside boats at marks or obstructions, give them room." Rule 42.1(a)(i) says this and adds detail:

An outside yacht shall give each yacht **overlapping** her on the inside room to round or pass the **mark** or **obstruction**, except as provided in rules 42.1(a)(iii), and (iv) and 42.3. Room includes room for an **overlapping** yacht to **tack** or **jibe** when either is an integral part of the rounding or passing maneuver.

The definition "Clear Astern and Clear Ahead; Overlap" ordinarily applies only to same-tack boats. However, for rule 42, boats can be on opposite tacks. The exception is at windward marks; this is the reference to rule 42.1(a)(iii) above. Later we will consider this and the other two exceptions, and how starting marks are affected.

Provision for giving room meets criteria for both safety and equity, although in practice, because there is a turn involved when boats pass a mark, the boat inside gains distance. Thus safety is somewhat better served than equity. Note that the rule does not give an insider right-of-way; it only gives her "room to round or pass." Therefore, when the outsider is an L, she retains her basic rights, under rule 37.1, over the insider, W.

How much room is required? Taking the two extreme possibilities, it might be all the room the insider might like in order to make a textbook rounding, or it might be the bare minimum needed for her to squeak through. The IYRU Rules Committee realized this problem when confronted with two appeals that contradicted one another, and the result was IYRU 40. It answers the question, saying room "means the room needed by an inside yacht, which, in the prevailing conditions, is handled in a seamanlike manner, to pass in safety between an outside yacht and a mark or obstruction."

The key words and phrases are "prevailing conditions," "seamanlike manner," and "safety." Imagine the difference between ghosting along in two knots of wind on perfectly flat water, and planing down toward a leeward mark which is being tossed to and fro by thirty-five knots of wind and four-foot waves. Yet even the latter conditions do not allow the insider all the room in the world; her skipper is expected to handle her well (although not expertly) in making the rounding. Case 40 does not provide a precise definition of "room," but it seems clear that the inside boat cannot expect to round as she might if she were there alone. Yet she should be allowed to round without fear of hitting the mark or the boat next to her, and without having to jam herself into such a tight turn that she loses considerable headway.

When tacking or jibing is the logical thing to do, "room" allows space for such a maneuver also, and thus makes an exception to rule 41.1, which would otherwise require a boat changing tack to keep clear. This does not permit an insider to decide to tack at a reaching mark because she is afraid to jibe in a strong wind. At such a mark jibing would be considered "an integral part" of the rounding, but a tack would not.

Note that rule 42.1 does not prescribe any minimum distance between two boats, as, for example, rule 38.2 does by limiting the definition of an overlap. Given the basic definition in Part I, boats can be overlapped while considerable distances apart, and they can be approaching a mark at quite different course angles. Here are some of the possibilities:

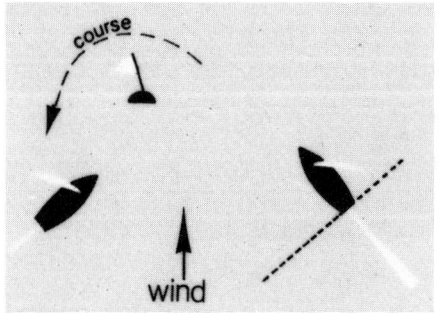

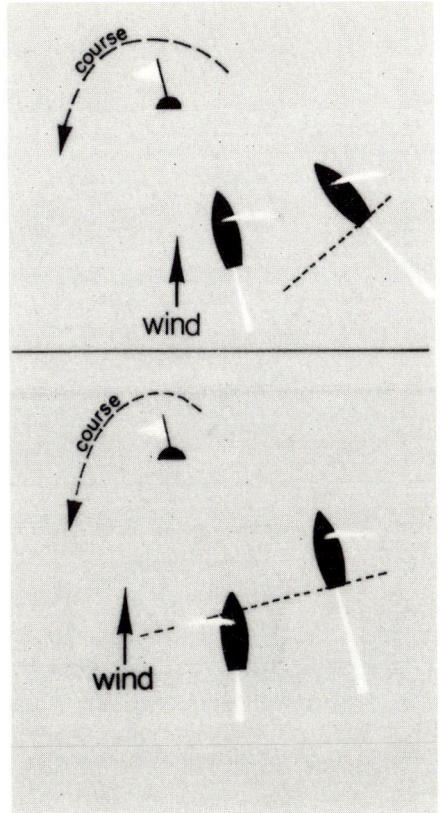

When there are three or more boats, an important sentence in the "overlap" definition comes into play:

The yachts **overlap** if . . . although one is **clear astern**, an intervening yacht overlaps both of them.

An outsider may have to give room to several boats, each connected to the next with an overlap, the entire connection binding the most outside boat:

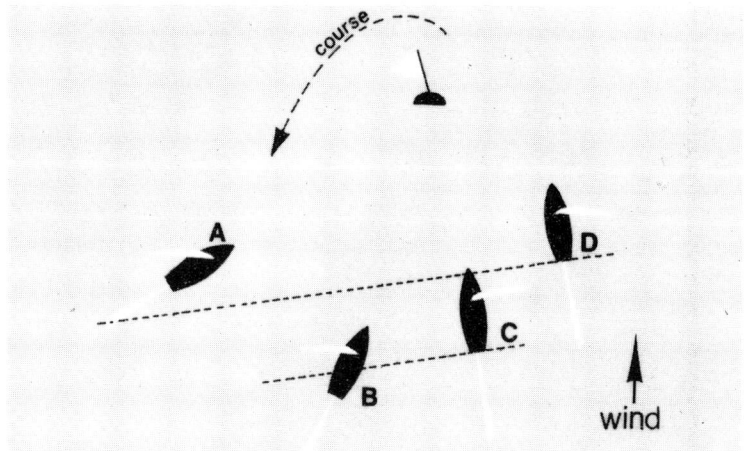

Boat D must give room to A and C because they overlap her directly, but she also must give it to B because C is an "intervening" boat, which is overlapped with both B and D.

Check your dictionary to see what "intervening" means, then consider IYRU 59. Three boats approached a mark, as shown here. However, C was traveling much faster and was about to overlap A on the inside:

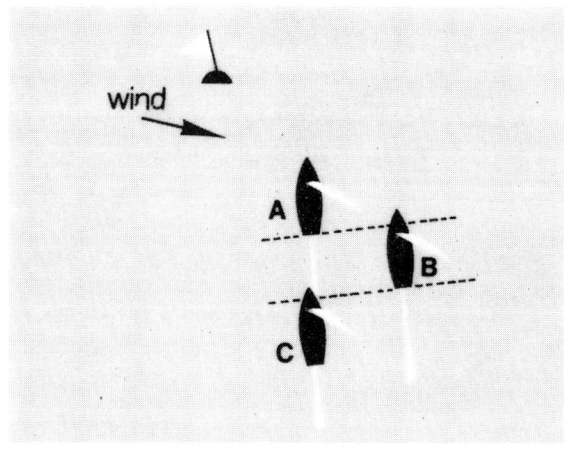

A and B are overlapped; so are B and C. B must give room to C. Must A also give room to C?

The answer is no, because B is not an intervening boat, at least in the eyes of the rules authorities. True, she lies between A and C in a course-wise direction, but not laterally. To be "intervening," an intermediate boat's course must lie between the courses of the other boats:

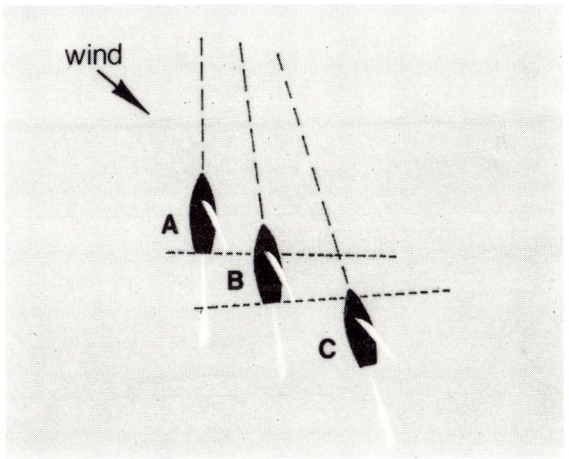

Here, A and C are overlapped because B overlaps each of them and her course makes her an intervening boat.

Rule 42.1(a)(ii) prohibits the inside boat from exercising some of the other rights she otherwise would have under rule 36 or 37.1:

> When an inside yacht of two or more **overlapped** yachts either on opposite **tacks**, or on the same **tack** without **luffing** rights, will have to **jibe** in order most directly to assume a **proper course** to the next **mark**, she shall **jibe** at the first reasonable opportunity.

Thus an inside starboard-tack boat must jibe rather than carry an outside port-tack boat off course:

74 — The Yacht Racing Rules Today

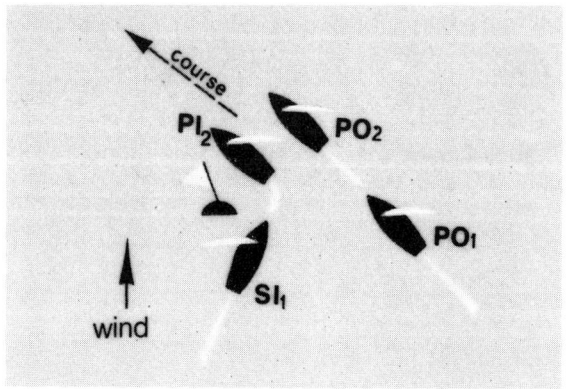

and a leeward boat, inside, must also jibe rather than force the outside windward boat off course (unless she has rule 38.1's special luffing rights):

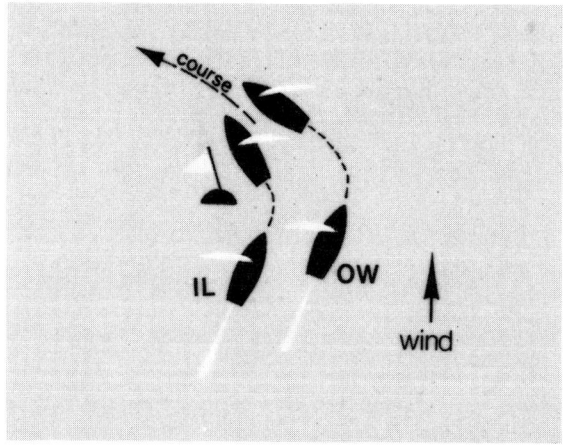

Here is an exception to rules 36 and 37. While it has been held (RYA 73/4) that a leeward boat without luffing rights is required to jibe because she would otherwise be sailing above her (new) proper course, the easiest way to consider the matter is to think of rule 42.1(a)(ii) as an exception to rule 37.1, requiring L to make way for W.

Notice that 42.1(a)(ii) is not an exception to rule 38.1. If L has "luffing rights" (meaning her special 38.1 luffing rights and not her right to luff within the limits of her proper course) she may luff W, or bear off without jibing, as she prefers.

The phrase "*most directly* to assume a **proper course** to the next **mark**" (italics added) is somewhat muddy in that if a boat's proper course were in fact to remain on the same tack for a while, her course on that tack would be assumed "most directly" as soon as she assumed it. The rule is trying to say that she must jibe and steer generally toward the next mark if the straight-line course to that mark would require her to jibe. Also, she must jibe at the "first reasonable opportunity"; this is somewhat vague, but it means that she must jibe without any unusual delay. If there are boats inside her, this would delay her "reasonable opportunity" to jibe.

Several of the rules under 42 amplify or limit the basic provisions of 42.1(a)(i). For example, 42.1(b)(i) requires the boat clear astern to "keep clear in anticipation of and during the rounding or passing maneuver when the yacht **clear ahead** remains on the same **tack** or **jibes.**" If there is no overlap when the lead boat "is about to round or pass," any overlap created by the turn itself cannot be claimed by the boat astern as grounds for the right to have room to round inside. This is just a reminder that a boat astern, required to keep clear already by rule 37.2, must continue to keep clear during a mark-rounding. Note, too, that jibing is included as part of the rounding, but tacking, covered in rules 42.1(a)(iii) and 42.1(b)(ii), is not.

Perhaps the most important of these supplemental rules about "the right to room" is the two-length circle rule,

42.2(a)(i). It says the boat astern may not have room "when the yacht **clear ahead** (i) is within two of her overall lengths of the **mark** or **obstruction**." The two lengths distance defines a space, and the space can be considered a circle, since there is no limit to the directions from which boats may be approaching the mark. (See illustrations on pages 70–71 for some of the possibilities.) By defining a space, the rule thereby provides for a certain amount of time, although on windy days in fast boats the time is obviously much less than on drifting days in slow boats. The main point is that the two-length limit is an arbitrary measurement that helps decide whether an inside boat may claim room.

Don't make the mistake of thinking that rule 42 applies only when the leading boat reaches the two-length circle. Rule 42.2(a)(i) provides only the minimum distance at which 42.1(a)(i) comes into play. In that rule, which mentions yachts "about to round or pass" a mark or obstruction, the phrase "about to" can and should be interpreted broadly. Consider, for example, two Tornado cats in twenty knots of wind as they approach a leeward mark. They are "about to" round that mark long before the leader hits the circle.

This explains the need for part (ii) of rule 42.2(a), which says there is no right to room if the lead boat "is *unable* to give the required room" (italics added). "Unable" is a strong word, and a broad one. In our Tornado example it would apply, because even with five or six lengths to go, an outside boat would find it virtually impossible to change course abruptly in time to make room for the insider. If they were passing to windward of a mark, the course change could easily result in a capsize.

Another reason a boat might be unable to give room is that, by turning away from the mark, she would close the space between her and the mark by swinging her stern; or, there might be a third boat outside her that does not respond in time to the arrival of the new insider. Thus, although the two-length circle helps protect a boat ahead, she is also helped by the "unable to give" clause.

In NAYRU 53, two Ps were running, inside an S, toward a mark. When more than four lengths from the mark, S and the nearest P touched. P was disqualified because the boats were not yet "about to" round, and the two-length circle concept was applied in support of this view. Thus, we cannot assume that the "about to round" requirement always comes into play at a greater distance than two lengths from the mark. Each situation requires a separate judgment.

RYA 66/10 illustrates the problems a late arrival has, in a group rounding a mark. Four boats were involved, the first three overlapped. The fourth came from astern and established an overlap on the closest boat before that boat was inside the circle. However, the outermost boat had already entered the circle. Since the latecomer made her overlap after the outsider entered the circle, it was too late for her to claim room from any of the others. This is one effect of the "overlap" definition's provisions that two boats are considered overlapped when an intervening boat overlaps them both.

Another fine point is that 42.2(a)(i) applies when the leading boat "*is within*" the circle. If she enters but then leaves the circle, as she might when a foul tide is running behind boats that are attempting to round a leeward mark, the boat behind has every right to cut inside her.

This brings us to rule 42.2(d)(i):

A yacht **clear ahead** shall be under no obligation to give room to a yacht **clear astern** before an **overlap** is established.

Even when the boat ahead sees one astern of her moving faster, she need not worry about a last-minute obligation arising as long as there is no overlap when she reaches the two-length circle. Part ii of the same rule puts the onus on the boat astern to show that she had her overlap "in proper time." This is added protection for the boat ahead. "Proper time" means either before the other boat reaches the circle or in time for the other boat to be "able" to give room in the context of rule 42.2(a)(ii), just discussed.

Rule 42.2(e)(i) complements 42.2(d)(i) by covering the case where an overlap did exist at the circle but was broken immediately afterward:

> When an outside yacht is **overlapped** at the time she comes within two of her overall lengths of the **mark** or an **obstruction**, she shall continue to be bound by rule 42.1(a)(i) to give room as required even though the **overlap** may thereafter be broken.

Its part (ii) also provides an onus; it is on the outside boat to show that the overlap was broken in time. Here the insider that had an overlap during the approach is protected.

An easy way to remember the above two onus-rule applications is to remember that, in a doubtful situation, the boat that claimed that circumstances changed at the last minute is the boat with the onus to show otherwise. If there had been no overlap, the boat claiming she had established one at the last minute must argue convincingly. Similarly, if there had been an overlap, the boat claiming she had broken it at the last minute must do the convincing.

NAYRU 87, later IYRU 5, is an interesting case showing how the two-length circle can apply. In the diagram, I has entered the circle ahead of O, even though O is clear ahead:

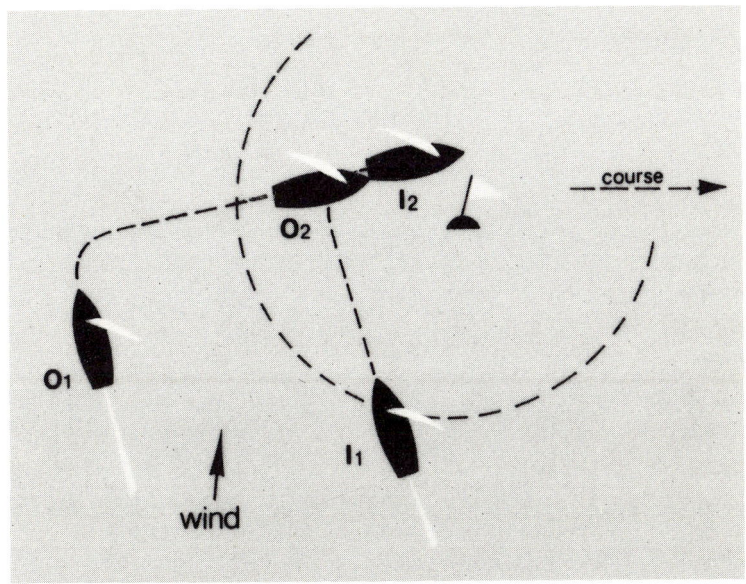

This was possible because O was some distance from the mark laterally. After both jibed, O struck I from astern. Rule 42 gave I victory in this case, because when I became overlapped by O at the time O turned to jibe, she was already inside the circle. Thus O was obligated to give I room to round. (Fundamental rule 37.2 protected I also, although the appeals committee omitted any mention of this.)

A special tactical weapon is provided by rule 42.1(a)(iv), which allows a leeward boat with 38.1 luffing rights to carry another boat the wrong side of a mark:

An outside **leeward yacht** with luffing rights may take an inside yacht to windward of a **mark** provided that she hails to that effect and begins to **luff** before she is within two of her overall lengths of the **mark** and provided that she also passes to windward of it.

80 – The Yacht Racing Rules Today

This rule can apply only when passing a mark to windward would take the boats the wrong side of a mark. This would be the case when, for example, in sailing the standard Olympic course, two port-tack boats approach the windward mark on or above the port-tack lay line. More commonly it would apply at leeward marks, and at finish-line marks. Because rule 38's luffing rights can usually be exercised without warning, the hailing requirement of 42.1(a)(iv) is important.

The phrase "to windward" in rule 42.1(a)(iv) is one whose meaning can be found only in the appeals. It does not mean "to windward" in the ordinary sense; it means "going past the mark on the wrong side." How far past? That point is determined by drawing a perpendicular across the direct course from the last mark:

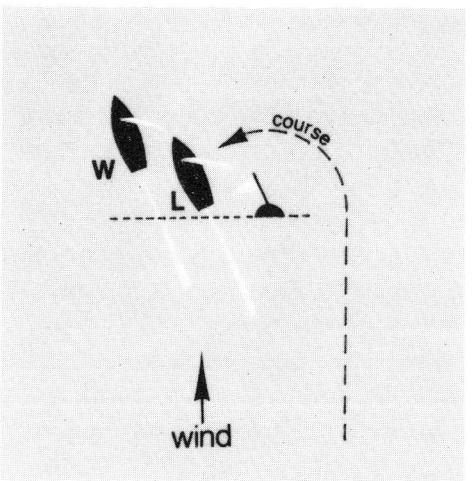

Here the leeward boat has only just met the rule's requirement that she "also passes to windward" of the mark. Notice that the luff must begin before the leeward boat reaches the two-length circle. Theoretically, this means the windward boat could have entered the circle already, if she were slightly ahead of the other but still abaft the "mast abeam" position. Potentially, this rule offers a serious hazard to any inside boat that is close aboard an outsider who has 38.1 rights.

Several interesting appeals involve rule 42.1(a)(iv). In NAYRU 57, diagramed here, the perpendicular-line test is made explicit, which makes that appeal a direct source of part of the rules:

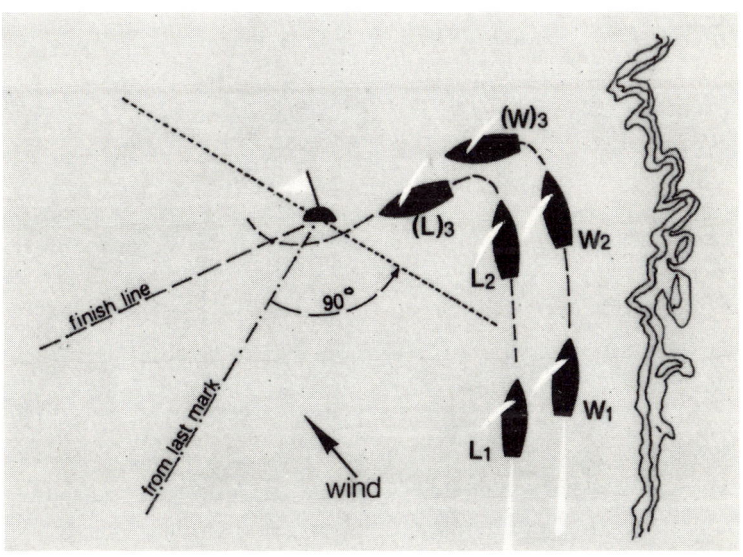

Two starboard tackers had sailed well high of the finish line which ended a reaching leg, and the leeward boat jibed to cross the line while the windward boat went beyond the finish line before returning. W's protest was disallowed because the leeward boat had met all requirements of 42.1(a)(iv), including the fact that "her course took her past a line through the mark *normal* to her direct course to it" (italics added). "Normal" here means perpendicular. This case is especially interesting because both boats approached the line from an odd angle in relation to the previous mark, and the finish line was very nearly parallel to the last leg's course. This doubtless added to the windward boat's (and the overruled race committee's) confusion.

NAYRU 58 shows how dangerous this rule can be. Two Lightnings, sailing in 25 mph winds and rough seas, neared a mark that ended a close-reaching leg. L hailed and luffed when only three lengths from the mark. W did not respond, thinking that rule 42's basic provisions granted her the right to claim room to pass the mark. But since L still had rule 38 luffing rights, she was entitled to use rule 42.1(a)(iv) at any time before reaching the edge of the circle. Thus, although the "about to round or pass" requirement of rule 42.1 can come into play before a lead boat reaches the circle—and usually does—a leeward boat's 38.1 luffing rights coupled with 42.1(a)(iv) can override a windward boat's expectation of receiving room as prescribed by 42.1(a)(i). Here is one illustration of one rule of Section E overriding an earlier rule of the same section.

In NAYRU 145 (later IYRU 55), the relationship between 38.1 and 42.1(a)(iv) is discussed in reply to questions asked by a race committee. The appeals committee noted that there is no exact point at which a boat can be said to be "about to round or pass" in rule 42's terms, although the two-length circle determines when an overlap must exist, if 42.1(a)(i) is to apply. However, as we have noted, the boats may well be about to round before that stage, and a leeward boat, if she plans to use 42.1(a)(iv), must hail and start her luff before that stage. But since 38.1 requires no hail, and 42.1(a)(iv) does, when is a hail required? The answer must be a matter of judgment by the protest committee as to when the boats were "about to round"; after that point the hail requirement applies. If in doubt, you had best hail when about to luff, if there is a mark nearby. This does not commit you to going to the wrong side of the mark, as long as you leave room for W once you bear off for the mark yourself. In W's place, remember that if L has 38.1 luffing rights, you are vulnerable under 42.1(a)(iv) until L enters the two-length circle.

About rule 42's applicability to continuing obstructions: although it does apply in its fundamental provisions, some important details do not. There is no two-length circle provision (see rule 42.2(a)(i), which makes 42.2(c) an exception). Thus, except for the "unable to give the required room" clause in 42.2(a)(ii), an overtaking boat can claim an overlap and room rights any time before the outside boat reaches the obstruction. However, rule 42.2(e) *does* apply. If an overlap is broken after the boat ahead is inside the circle, the boat behind may still claim room.

At Windward Marks

Rule 42 deals with windward marks also, but certain exceptions apply. Considering windward marks separately seems to make for easier understanding. Don't make the mistake of thinking that "Room-at-the-mark doesn't apply at windward marks," as is sometimes heard. Sometimes it does, sometimes it doesn't.

Rule 42.1(a)(iii) says that 42.1(a)(i) will not apply to boats "on opposite tacks . . . on a beat." It refers to rules 36 and 41. Rule 42.1(a)(iii) is the one that sometimes suggests that there is "no room" at weather marks. However, its only purpose is to state that rule 42 applies only to boats on the same tack, at windward marks. Here are two situations at windward marks where rule 42 does require an outsider to give an insider room:

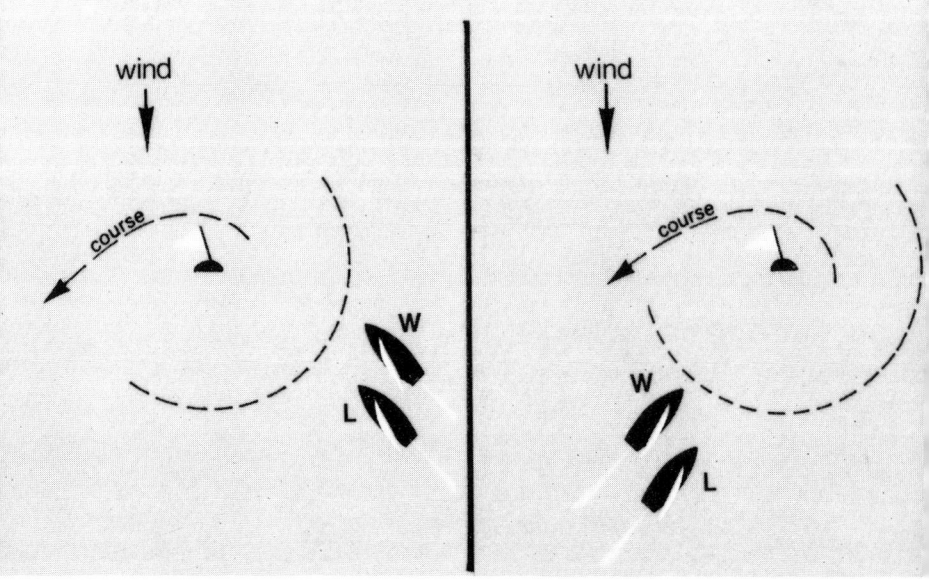

In each, assume that the windward boat is slightly above the lay line, and that in the starboard-tack case L will be able to round the mark without luffing beyond head-to-wind. The outsider must give room in both cases. In the port-tack case, this includes room to tack, since the tack is an "integral part of the rounding," as provided for in rule 42.1(a)(i).

One of the most interesting windward-mark rules is the one cancelling the two-length circle under certain circumstances, 42.2(b):

The two-lengths determinative above shall not apply to yachts, of which one has completed a **tack** within two overall lengths of a **mark** or an **obstruction**.

Several variations are possible. In all of them the key question is: Did one boat complete a tack inside the circle?

Consider the following, which is the case rule 42.2(b) was designed to govern:

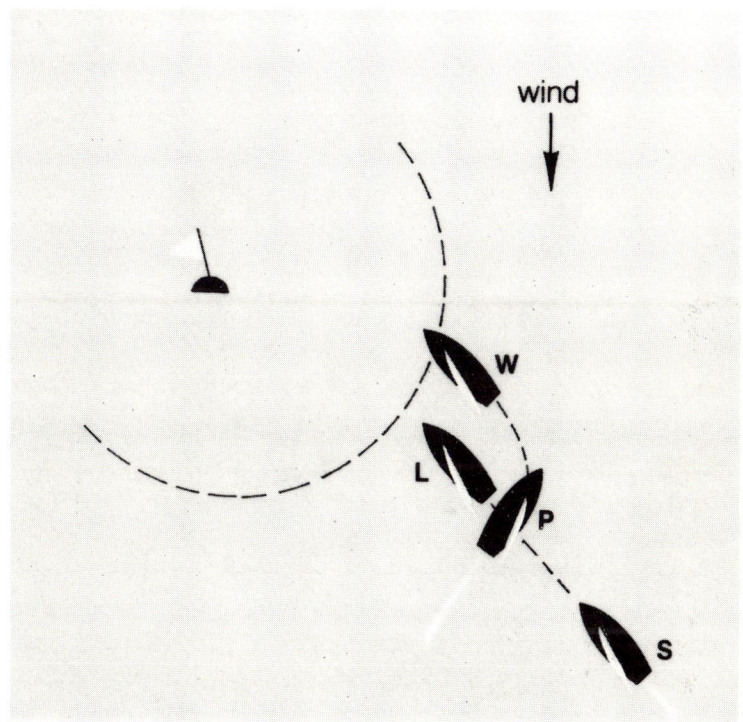

S is on the lay line, moving well. P crosses ahead of S, just before S reaches the circle, and tacks just to windward of her. Because P's tack has reduced her speed, S moves into an overlap but only after P has borne off to a close-hauled course, thus completing her tack. At this stage P's bow is inside the circle. Without rule 42.2(b), P, now W, would have no obligation to give S, now L, room. However, rule 37.1 protects L and at least prevents W from forcing her to alter course. This suggests that all of rule 42 is only of academic interest when applied to this situation, but in any event L is doubly protected.

In the following case, the two-length circle does not apply, because L did not come from clear astern (reread rule 42.2(a)), and L is totally dependent on her rights under rules 37.1 with an added assist from 38.1:

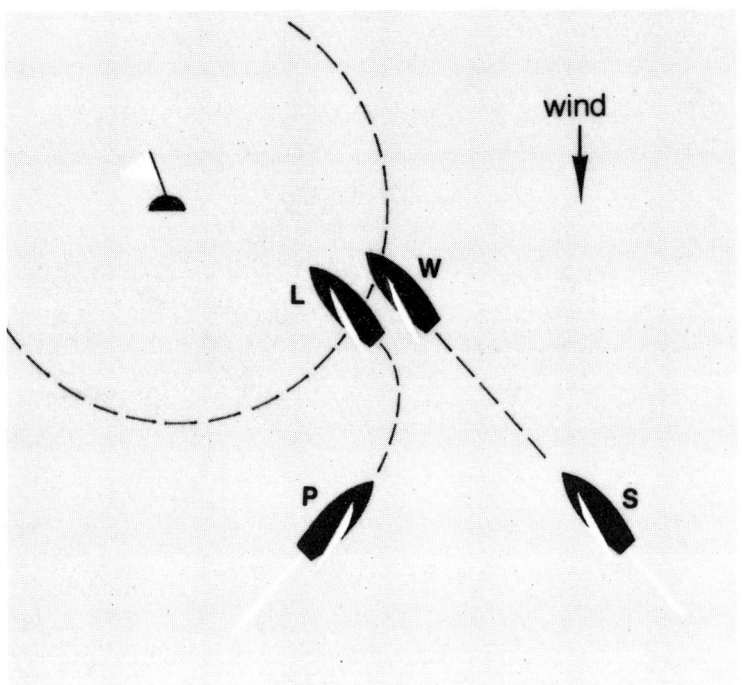

If by this time you feel slightly confused, this is understandable. Rule 42 makes exception to earlier rules. The two-length circle is a condition for 42's applicability, but there are exceptions to it. This means there are four layers of rules to remember when thinking about windward marks: (1) basic rules 36 and 37, (2) their sometimes being rendered inapplicable at marks, (3) the two-length circle requirement, and (4) its being rendered inapplicable part of the time.

Before leaving the windward mark and its problems, consider rule 42.1(b)(ii):

> A Yacht **clear ahead** which **tacks** to round a **mark** is subject to rule 41, Tacking or Jibing, but a yacht **clear astern** shall not **luff** above **close-hauled** so as to prevent the yacht **clear ahead** from tacking.

Although this rule can apply on offwind legs in rare instances (when the fleet is rounding a mark between two reaches in an upwind direction), it also can apply at a windward mark when two boats will have to tack to round the mark. Here, A is just able to tack and cross B if B does not luff, and the rule prohibits such a luff:

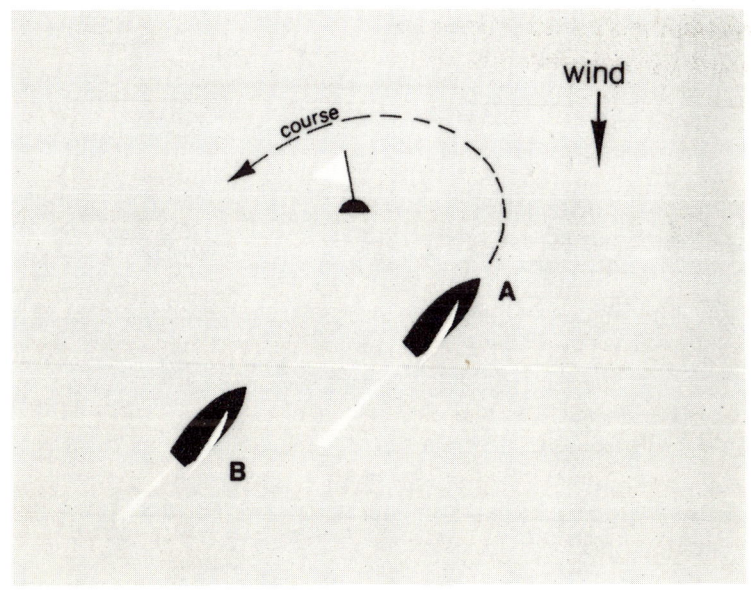

At Starting Marks

Rule 42.1's introductory paragraph has a phrase saying "with the exception of a starting **mark** surrounded by navigable water" to indicate that room to pass inside a starting mark cannot be claimed through rule 42. This means that the two-length circle is irrelevant, as is the entire question of whether an overlap was established in time.

There are three modifications of rule 42.1's cancellation of room rights, however. The first is rule 42.3, often called the "antibarging" rule, because it protects those boats making close-hauled approaches, at the end of the line, from others who are sailing courses less close to the wind. The other two modifications concern marks that are also obstructions, and marks that are obstructions not surrounded by navigable water.

Rule 42.3 softens the harshness of 42.1's removal of room rights by limiting a leeward boat's luffing rights while passing a starting mark. It can apply to starboard-tack boats crossing at the starboard end of the line, or port-tack boats crossing at the other end:

> When approaching the starting line to **start**, a **leeward yacht** shall be under no obligation to give any **windward yacht** room to pass to leeward of a starting **mark** surrounded by navigable water; but, after the starting signal, a **leeward yacht** shall not deprive a **windward yacht** of room at such a **mark** by sailing either above the course to the first **mark** or above **close-hauled**.

The first part merely reinforces 42.1 but makes it clear that even when the mark is an obstruction surrounded by navigable water—which is what race-committee boats are—a leeward boat need not give room to an inside windward boat. Before the starting signal she may luff head-to-wind to protect her wind or position. Rule 40's limitation against luffing above a close-hauled course does not apply, because of the preamble to Section E. However, 42.3 does *not* cancel 40's requirement that a luff be made "slowly." Once the starting signal is given L must bear off to a close-hauled course (assuming a windward leg), or to the straight-line course to the next mark. When past the mark, L is entitled to any luffing rights she may have under rule 38.1.

Rule 42.3 applies only when "approaching the starting line to **start**." So if the mark is an obstruction, be sure to give any overlapped boat room to pass it during pre-start maneuvering.

There is one tricky exception to 42.3's applicability. If the RC boat has a stern anchor set, the rule does not apply, because the anchor line is an obstruction but not part of the mark. Rule 42.1(a)(i) applies to obstructions, making exception only to those obstructions that are starting marks surrounded by navigable water. In such a case, an inside overlapped W can claim room to pass. After passing, she can still be luffed legally under rule 42.3, but by that time both boats are probably too far to leeward for L to make much use of 42.3.

At the port-end mark, the rights and obligations of two starboard tackers are defined by rules 37.1, 40; and, if the mark is a race-committee boat and therefore an obstruction, by rule 43 ("Close-Hauled, Hailing for Room to Tack at Obstructions"). We'll examine rule 43 shortly. For now, remember that L can luff under rule 40 before clearing the starting line, and that she has basic leeward-boat rights under rule 37.1.

In NAYRU 36, L overtook W as both approached the port end of the line, and W forced L to leeward of the mark. W was disqualified for infringing rule 37.1. The appeals committee also noted that L also had the right to luff W slowly, even though abaft the "mast abeam" position. Once past "mast abeam," she could luff above close-hauled.

If it happens that either end of the line is an obstruction not surrounded by navigable water—such as a dock or point of land—then rule 42.1(a)(i) applies without modification. The introductory paragraph of 42.1 makes an exception of a starting mark (which can include obstructions) surrounded by navigable water, but not of all obstructions. Rule 42.3 would not apply either, because it refers only to marks surrounded by navigable water.

The last rule affecting rights at starting marks is 43, concerned with room to tack at obstructions. It applies anywhere on the course. Therefore we will consider it broadly first, returning later to its implications at starting marks.

Room to Tack at Obstructions

One reason rule 43 applies at all times is that its purpose is safety. It allows a boat that needs to tack to avoid an obstruction the right to do so even though the rules otherwise would not allow this. The remedy provided is to require a nearby windward boat to make room for a leeward boat's tack. The rule sets specific requirements for both boats and also allows the boat being hailed to avoid the hailing boat by means other than tacking, or to challenge the hailing boat's need to use the rule. Rule 43 begins as follows:

Hailing. When two **close-hauled** yachts are on the same **tack** and safe pilotage requires the yacht **clear ahead** or the **leeward yacht** to make a substantial alteration of course to clear an **obstruction**, and if she intends to **tack**, but cannot **tack** without colliding with the other yacht, she shall hail the other yacht for room to **tack** and clear the other yacht, but she shall not hail and **tack** simultaneously.

Beyond the Basics—Part II – 91

Notice the many conditions that must exist if rule 43 is to apply. It considers only a two-boat relationship, and both must be on the same tack. Clearing the obstruction will require a *substantial* alteration of course. L must be unable to tack and clear W without colliding with her. (If L can tack and then clear W by bearing off, she must do so.) If all this is true, then L must (1) hail, but (2) must allow time for a response that is prescribed in 42.2:

Responding. The hailed yacht at the earliest possible moment after the hail shall either:—
(a) **tack**, in which case the hailing yacht shall begin to **tack** either:—
   (i) before the hailed yacht has completed her **tack**, or
   (ii) if she cannot then **tack** without colliding with the hailed yacht, immediately she is able to **tack** and clear her, or
(b) reply "You **tack**," or words to that effect, if in her opinion she can keep clear without **tacking** or after postponing her **tack**. In this case:—
   (i) the hailing yacht shall immediately **tack** and
   (ii) the hailed yacht shall keep clear.
   (iii) The onus shall lie on the hailed yacht which replied "You **tack**" to satisfy the race committee that she kept clear.

The hailed boat must respond immediately, either by tacking or with a hail. Either way, L is then free to tack as soon as she can do so and clear W. If W tacks, L must tack right away, and definitely before W completes her tack, unless W was so close that L must wait for W to make more room. All these provisions are meant to protect W by preventing L from hailing her about and then sailing farther on the old tack to her own advantage.

If W believes L has room to tack and clear her, or wants to delay tacking and thinks she can do so and still clear L, she should hail "You tack." She thereby takes on the obligation of keeping clear of L either by tacking later or by simply holding her course. (By virtue of her initial position, she may be free from having to tack.) Note that if she makes this choice she has the onus of satisfying the committee that she did keep clear without causing the other boat to take avoiding action.

One of the most common applications of rules 43.1 and 43.2 is when the obstruction is a right-of-way boat:

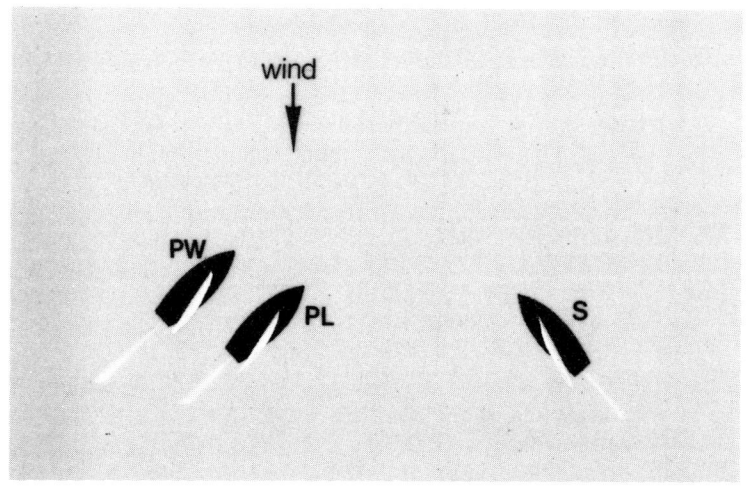

Assume S's position requires a "substantial alteration of course" by PL, required for rule 43 to apply. PL is entitled to either bear off around S's stern or exercise her right to hail PW for room to tack. The choice is not PW's. Under 42.1(a)(i), only if PL decides to go astern of S can PW claim room to pass between the two. PL is given the choice by the phrase "if" she intends to tack, in 43.1, and also because rule 43 takes precedence over 42 wherever they conflict. This is prescribed in the preamble to Section E. Any rule in the section takes precedence over any earlier conflicting rule (except those in Part A), including earlier rules of Section E.

Various appeals show how rule 43 works. In NAYRU 147, L hailed but got no answer from W, and so tacked and hit W. She testified that she had received "no response" from W. L lost her case. The committee agreed that L's judgment as to her safety must be accepted in the absence of facts found which would "*prove* otherwise" (italics added); and further, that W's failing to hear L's hail did not relieve her of her obligations. However, the committee also decided that L had not fulfilled her requirement to hail, in that she had hailed only once. Thus L's hail must be adequate. The rule requires only one hail, and has no other requirement of "adequate notice." Thus, this is another appeal that makes an additional rule: an "adequate" hail is required, which may include a second hail if the first elicits no response.

In NAYRU 81, L hailed, W did not respond, and L tacked anyway. This time, W kept clear. It was decided that L's action was permissible, even though she was not entitled to tack until W's response, as per 43.2, because W had failed to do her part under 43.2. On the other hand, W was held blameless also. Although she violated 43.2 by failing to respond, she did keep clear. Thus, here is an interesting precedent for a rule infringement going unpenalized as long as the harm that the rule was designed to avoid was in fact avoided.

In RYA 64/26, L hailed and then tacked almost immediately. She was disqualified for failing to give W adequate time to respond. The moral: when you are L, allow sufficient time for W's response before you arrive at the obstruction.

In RYA 65/15, L hailed, tacked onto port tack, and hit W. She could have gone below W. Since the rule applies only when L cannot tack *and clear* the other, L lost her case.

Notice the precise time at which L must tack in relation

to W's tack. L must begin to tack before W completes hers. W's tack is complete when she is on a close-hauled course; L's does not begin until she is slightly beyond head-to-wind. If both tack at the same rate of speed, L must start luffing for her tack no later than the time at which W is head-to-wind. The exception is when the two are so close together that L cannot tack until W has moved away on her new tack.

W should keep in mind the tactical advantage of delaying her tack, by hailing "You tack." If W can keep clear by tacking after L's tack, she may want to use that option so that she will be further to windward afterward.

Rule 43.3 covers the special case of an obstruction that is also a mark. A race-committee boat anchored at the port end of the starting line is one example. Consider it, in studying this rule:

Limitation on Right to Room when the Obstruction is a Mark.
 (a) When the hailed yacht can fetch an **obstruction** which is also a **mark**, the hailing yacht shall not be entitled to room to **tack** and clear the other yacht and the hailed yacht shall immediately so inform the hailing yacht.
 (b) If, thereafter, the hailing yacht again hails for room to **tack** and clear the other yacht she shall, after receiving it, retire immediately.
 (c) If, after having refused to respond to a hail under rule 43.3(a), the hailed yacht fails to fetch, she shall retire immediately.

The net effect of this rule is to make things extremely risky for L if she approaches too close to an obstruction that is also a mark. She can force W to tack, if necessary, but at the high cost of disqualification or other prescribed penalty. There is a risk that W takes, too, if she decides she can lay the mark and hails L accordingly. If W fails to fetch, she must accept the penalty.

At the start, then, L can hail for room to tack if neither L nor W can fetch the RC boat:

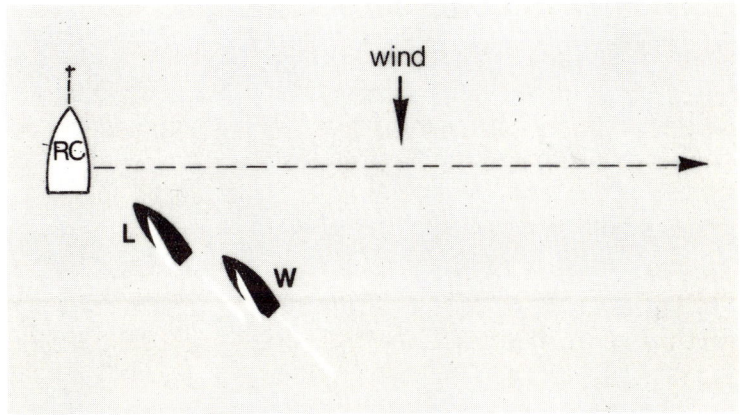

However, if W can lay it and safely cross its anchor line, L's only recourse is to slow down in advance until W has passed; or, if that is no longer possible, to hail W for room and then take the penalty. As in so many situations, it is important to see circumstances building up before it is too late.

Other Obstructions

All of the discussion of rule 42's various subsections under this book's "At Marks—Off the Wind" section (page 68) applies also to obstructions that are not marks of the course, with the exception noted there: the two-length-circle provision does not apply to continuing obstructions.

Reread the definition of obstruction:

An **obstruction** is any object, including craft under way, large enough to require a yacht, if not less than one overall length away from it, to make a substantial alteration of course to pass on one side or the other, or any object which can be passed on one side only, including a buoy when the yacht in question cannot safely pass between it and the shoal or object which it marks.

"Substantial" is necessarily vague, as is "safely" when used in the last part of the rule. In practice, these words have not caused serious interpretation problems. By limiting the distance from the obstruction to a minimum of one boat length, the size of the obstruction is related to the size of the yacht. Another boat of the same class would easily qualify; for small boats some large government marks would also qualify, although for larger boats they might not.

We have already seen that other boats in the same race can be obstructions—so can boats in another race, or boats not racing at all, including committee boats, commercial vessels, or spectator boats. For obstructions not surrounded by navigable water, special rules apply. The only remaining type of obstruction referred to in the rules is a continuing obstruction, and rule 42.2 (c) applies:

> A yacht **clear astern** may establish an **overlap** between the yacht **clear ahead** and a continuing **obstruction** such as a shoal or the shore, only when there is room for her to do so in safety.

If there is a dispute, whether the judgment of "safety" is to be accepted from the inside boat or the outside boat becomes an important question. Unfortunately, except for one or two outdated British appeals, there is no case law guidance to suggest the answer. On the one hand, the judgment of the outside, clear-ahead boat might be given greatest weight. The wording of the rule suggests that the boat clear astern should attempt an overlap only if safety is not in doubt, and the boat ahead is presumably in a better position to observe the distance to the obstruction. On the other hand, it is the safety of the insider that is in question, and it might be held that she is the best judge of it. Fortunately, race committees usually try to avoid setting courses near continuing obstructions.

Changing Course

Several rules include prescriptions that allow or restrict changes in course: the two luffing-rights rules 38 and 40; rule 39, "Sailing Below a Proper Course"; and rule 41.1–3, "Tacking or Jibing," being four of the most important ones we have already seen. Here we will look at one of the most important rules in Part IV, rule 34, "Right-of-Way Yacht Altering Course." Rule 35, "Hailing," and 41.4 are also included.

This is rule 34:

When one yacht is required to keep clear of another, the right-of-way yacht shall not so alter course as to prevent the other yacht from keeping clear, or so as to obstruct her while she is keeping clear, except:
(a) to the extent permitted by rule 38.1, Right-of-Way Yacht Luffing after Starting, and
(b) when assuming a **proper course** to **start**, unless subject to the second part of rule 44.1(b), Yachts Returning to Start.

The first part of this rule lists three kinds of effects that a right-of-way boat's course change may have on another boat which is obligated to keep clear. If any one of them occurs, the right-of-way boat has infringed the rule. Note that other action on her part which might cause trouble for the other boat—such as slowing down, or speeding up—is not prohibited. Only a course change can cause legal trouble.

To prevent the other boat from keeping clear means that the right-of-way boat actually causes a collision. This could happen on a windward leg when a port tacker is successfully crossing ahead of S, but S then luffs and strikes P. To "obstruct" the other boat without a collision is physically less serious, but is just as serious as a rule violation. The *Concise Oxford Dictionary* (4th ed.), defines "obstruct" as "impede; prevent or retard progress of." Taken together, both mean that when a non right-of-way boat is in the process of keeping clear, either by changing course or by holding her course while close to the right-of-way boat, the right-of-way boat must not change her course in such a way that the other is hindered in any way.

The appeals show the rule in action, along with some of the other rules. In RYA 72/2, P, on a windward leg, was passing astern of S when S tacked. In tacking, S swung her stern in a clockwise direction, which had the effect of making P delay her return to a close-hauled course. Since this caused an increase in the course alteration that otherwise would have sufficed for P, this increased course alteration was considered to be evidence of obstruction, and S was disqualified.

IYRU 35 is an answer to a question submitted by the U.S.S.R. yacht-racing organization. P and S are running side by side on parallel courses:

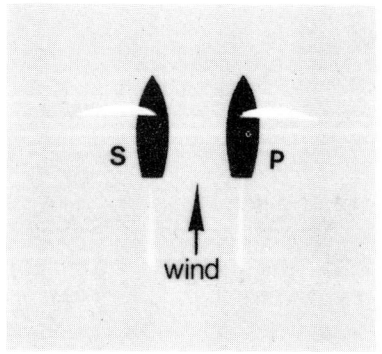

Beyond the Basics—Part II – 99

S hails and then luffs toward P and they touch. Does rule 36 work against P, or rule 34 against S, or both? The answer is that P has infringed rule 36 but S has not infringed rule 34. S cannot luff "as she pleases"; that is permissible only under 38.1 when boats are on the same tack. P has not been caught unaware; she has been the obligated boat for some time and has been warned by S's hail. Thus, although rule 34 limits S's movement to some extent, it does not prevent her from exercising her basic freedom of movement as a starboard-tack boat.

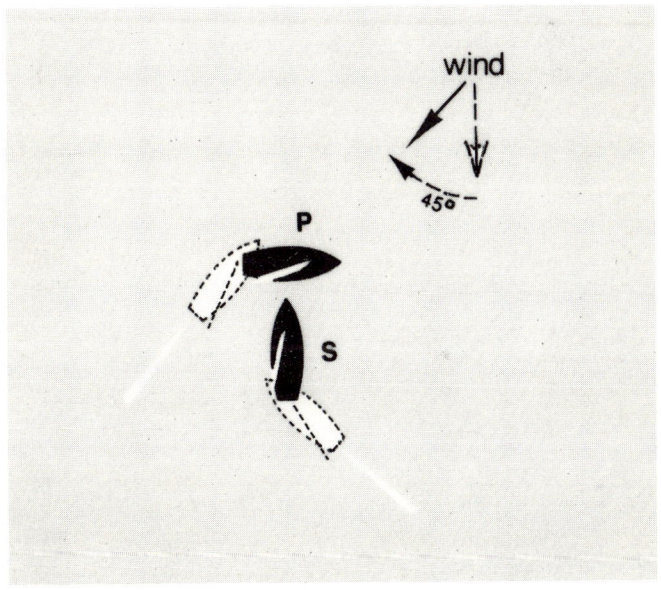

In another windward-leg case, IYRU 52, P is crossing ahead of S with no difficulty when a major wind shift heads her and lifts S so that S must bear off around P's stern to avoid a collision. Neither boat has infringed any rule. P was keeping clear when S luffed, so she did not violate rule 36. S might have violated rule 34 by luffing when so close to P, but since she bore off without bothering P, she too was guilty of no infringement.

As mentioned before, the concept of "keeping clear" means not only avoiding a collision but avoiding such a close shave that another boat is not frightened into taking some avoiding action. The same principle applies under rule 34: the right-of-way boat must not provoke the other into taking avoiding action by changing course too close aboard the other.

Two other appeals are of interest. In IYRU 10, P, on a windward leg, bore off astern of S and S tacked. P's protest was disallowed because in this case S's course change violated neither rule 41 nor 34. It did not obstruct P by costing her any additional course change, nor was she "prevented from" keeping clear—there was no collision. Rule 34 does not require the right-of-way boat to hold her course, as the Russian case already has shown. The common hail "Hold your course!" may be good gamesmanship but there is no specific obligation to hold one's course anywhere in the rules.

NAYRU 63 is a case where a *non* right-of-way boat obstructs a right-of-way boat, and this is permissible. In a series of match-race prestart maneuvers, a boat that is clear astern luffs as the boat ahead luffs, thus preventing the other from tacking.

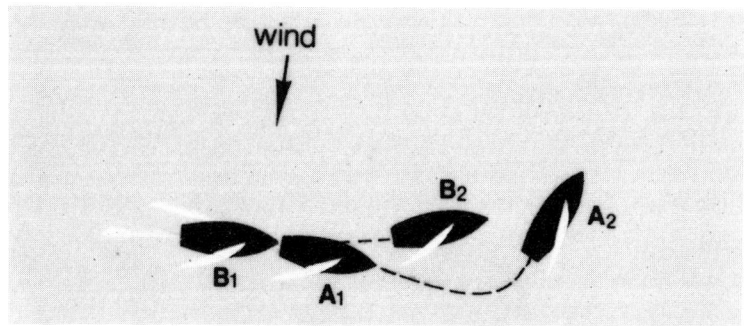

Beyond the Basics—Part II – 101

As the boat astern and then as the windward boat, B is the non right-of-way boat. She always meets her obligation to keep clear of A, who holds right-of-way first as a boat clear ahead and then as a leeward boat, but by luffing to windward of A she makes it impossible for A to tack. They are so close that, in tacking, A would infringe rule 41.1 by tacking too close.

One of two exceptions to rule 34 is 38, "Right-of-Way Yacht Luffing after Starting," which is an exception to several other rules as well. When a leeward boat has these special luffing rights she has virtually no limitations on making course changes, so long as she remains on the same tack. Rule 34 is then cancelled.

The second exception to rule 34 applies at the start and is a much less effective exception than first appears. It provides that "when assuming a **proper course** to **start,**" a right-of-way boat is not limited by rule 34. This is meant to protect a starboard tacker, reaching down the line, that wants to luff to a close-hauled course to make her start even though there is a P approaching from her left. It might look like this:

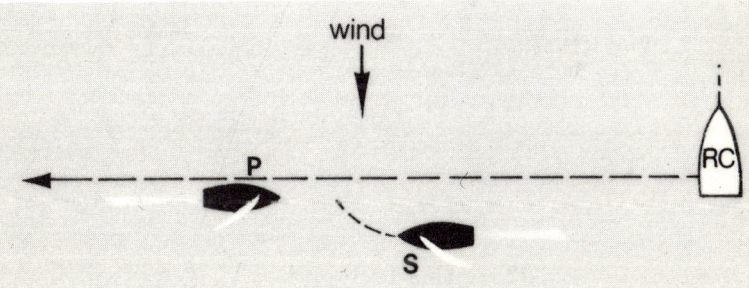

If rule 34 applied, P would be considered to be keeping clear, since her course would take her above S if S held her course. If S luffed, causing P to change course, S would thereby infringe 34. The exception is a warning to port tackers that at the start they must expect starboard tackers to head for the line and therefore avoid them.

At first glance 34(b) seems a good protection for a right-of-way boat that is preparing to make a valid start. However there is an unobvious hazard. S must be "assuming a **proper course** to **start**." But a proper course cannot exist until after the start signal; the final sentence of the definition of "proper course" says so. Thus 34(b) cannot protect S unless she is late in making her start; if the start signal is given before she has luffed to a close-hauled course, she has delayed too long. If her timing is good, on the other hand, she is still vulnerable, under 34, when she takes up her close-hauled course.

In practice it seems that most Ps instinctively accept S's "right" to take up a close-hauled course, and have not pressed their case under rule 34.

Rule 35, "Hailing," is a "carrot-and-stick" rule. It warns of penalties if one fails to hail, and holds out rewards for hailing. Neither the penalties nor the rewards are sizable, however. The penalty part says:

1. Except when **luffing** under rule 38.1, Right-of-Way Yacht Luffing after Starting, a right-of-way yacht which does not hail before or when making an alteration of course which may not be foreseen by the other yacht may be disqualified as well as the yacht required to keep clear when a collision resulting in serious damage occurs.

The idea is that a warning is a good thing (except when playing the special luffing-rights game), at least when an obligated boat may not be alert to a possible collision. For the right-of-way boat to be penalized, however, three conditions must be met. There is a serious collision, the right-of-way boat's course change could have gone unobserved by the other boat, and there was no hail from the right-of-way boat. Whether a collision is "serious" is open to debate, although IYRU 36 suggests some test questions for protest committees to use. Add the facts that the hail may be made *during* the right-of-way boat's course change and that the rule only allows, but does not require, her disqualification or penalization, and the weaknesses in the rule become clear.

The rewards for hailing come in part 2:

> A yacht which hails when claiming the establishment or termination of an **overlap** or insufficiency of room at a **mark** or **obstruction** thereby helps to support her claim for the purposes of rule 42, Rounding or Passing Marks and Obstructions.

The phrase "helps to support" means that your case will be strengthened in a hearing if you can show that you hailed, although hailing will not, by itself, win your case for you. Hailing at mark-rounding situations is a good idea for another reason; it informs the other boat exactly what you think your rights are, and by attracting the attention of other nearby boats it may provide you with a valuable witness if a protest and hearing come later. Notice that a hail by an outside boat that the insider is taking too much room is not mentioned, but presumably it would help to counter the value of any hail made by the inside boat that room was insufficient.

Rule 41.4 is the last of the rules to be considered in our "Changing Course" group. It says, "When two yachts are both **tacking** or both **jibing** at the same time, the one on the other's **port** side shall keep clear." Such a combination of events rarely occurs, but if it happens to you, remember that the right-hand boat is in the right. There is one problem of ambiguity; two boats can be tacking at the same time even though one has started before the other. This is because one boat can be nearing the end of her swing toward her new close-hauled course while the other is just passing beyond the head-to-wind position. Thus if two boats have just crossed, sailing to windward, and the starboard tacker starts to tack and is observed by the port tacker, the latter can start her tack and be tacking during a part of the time that the starboard tacker is still tacking. Does 41.4 protect the original port-tack boat and allow her to foil the other's attempt to tack?

RYA 69/9 covers such an encounter. S crossed ahead of P and began her tack, and P then began hers. The committee ruled that P violated 41.4 because she did not *start* to tack at the same time (yet another instance of making new rules in the appeals), but also because P violated rule 34 in that she "obstructed" S, who was in the act of keeping clear of P, as required by rule 41.1.

Correcting Errors

Rules 44 and 45 both allow one to correct his error by taking certain prescribed action. One covers premature starting and the other touching a mark. Rule 44.1(a) says:

A premature starter when returning to **start**, or a yacht working into position from the course side of the starting line or its extensions, when the starting signal is made, shall keep clear of all yachts which are **starting**, or have **started**, correctly, until she is wholly on the pre-start side of the starting line or its extensions.

The rule takes effect at the starting *signal*; before that time a boat across the line has any rights the rules afford her. It applies to boats across the extensions of the line also. As a practical matter such boats will not encounter others who have started or are starting properly, and the rule therefore has little effect outside the ends of the line.

This rule is often cited as one of the exceptions to the

starboard-over-port principle, though several other limitations on a starboard tacker's freedom of movement are found in the rules.

The next part of rule 44.1 says:

(b) Thereafter, she shall be accorded the rights under the rules of Part IV of a yacht which is **starting** correctly; but if she thereby acquires right of way over another yacht which is **starting** correctly, she shall allow that yacht ample room and opportunity to keep clear.

The last portion covers that time just after the early starter has returned for a valid start, and protects other boats nearby from immediately becoming obligated to a boat whose rights have suddenly reappeared. As we saw in rule 37.1, *ample room and opportunity* means "plenty," and the onus will be interpreted to be on the premature starter to show that she gave the other boat enough room or time to begin keeping clear after the premature starter returned below the line.

Rule 44.2 underlines the "when returning" phrase in rule 44.1(a), and is important because it emphasizes the moment at which the early starter loses her rights—it is not until she actually starts to return:

A premature starter while continuing to sail the course and until it is obvious that she is returning to **start**, shall be accorded the rights under the rules of Part IV of a yacht which has **started**.

Thus it can happen that a premature starter is boxed in by boats to windward and to leeward, and must first luff and slow down in order to be able to tack or jibe toward the starting line. If she slows down, or luffs, even head-to-wind, she is not yet *returning* to the line. She is only preparing to do so, even though it is clear to those around her that she has been recalled. The word "obvious" is an onus word; it means that if there is doubt, the jury will rule in favor of the premature starter who claims that she had not yet begun to return; to *go back*, literally.

Rule 45 is written in parallel fashion to 44:

1. A yacht which has touched a **mark**, and is about to exonerate herself in accordance with rule 52.2, Touching a Mark, shall keep clear of all other yachts which are about to round or pass it or have rounded or passed it correctly until she has rounded it completely and has cleared it and is on a **proper course** to the next **mark**.
2. A yacht which has touched a **mark** while continuing to sail the course and until it is obvious that she is returning to round it completly in accordance with rule 52.2, Touching a Mark, shall be accorded rights under the rules of Part IV.

In both rules 44 and 45, the boat in error must correct her mistake, and she loses her rights in the process, but only after she starts to *return* to do so. Also, the "obvious" stipulation protects her if there is doubt. The mark-toucher regains her rights only after she has "cleared" the mark—i.e., moved past it on a course that a normal rounding dictates, and is on some type of proper course on the new leg.

When Not Under Way

The above is Section F's title, and while its rules do not come into play often, they are nevertheless worth knowing. The entire section is rule 46:

1. A yacht under way shall keep clear of another yacht **racing** which is anchored, aground, or capsized. Of two anchored yachts, the one which anchored later shall keep clear, except that a yacht which is dragging shall keep clear of one which is not.

2. A yacht anchored or aground shall indicate the fact to any yacht which may be in danger of fouling her. Unless the size of the yachts or the weather conditions make some other signal necessary, a hail is sufficient indication.
3. A yacht shall not be penalized for fouling a yacht in distress which she is attempting to assist or a yacht which goes aground or capsizes immediately ahead of her.

The obligations between two anchored boats are only common sense; one anchoring later should leave room for the other to swing around, and if one of them is dragging she should be the one to take remedial action. A capsized boat presumably includes one that has come upright again, but is full of water or still out of control because her crew have not yet returned to their stations. A boat aground or anchored can still be on a tack (see the definition of "On a Tack"), and thus it happens that an anchored port tacker may have right-of-way over a starboard-tack boat. This might happen in a drifter when the fleet is fighting a current; the anchored boat may have her sails filled ready to take advantage of enough wind to move her up current. She must hail others that she is anchored, however.

The third part of rule 46 is another example where the rules protect a boat from having insufficient time to respond to a sudden change in another boat's rights. It also protects a boat that intends to give aid to another (as may be required by rule 58, "Rendering Assistance"), regardless of whether the boat in trouble has asked for help.

Some Basic Non Right-of-Way Provisions

Rules 31, 32, and 33 are not rules in the sense that they require a boat to do something. Yet they are important, because they explain the status of the other Part IV rules or the status of boats that have infringed the rules. Or, in the case of 32, they provide for penalizing a right-of-way boat.

Rule 31's subject is penalization, even though its title, "Disqualification," refers only to one form of penalization:

1. A yacht may be disqualified or otherwise penalized for infringing a rule of Part IV only when the infringement occurs while she is **racing**, whether or not a collision results.
2. A yacht may be disqualified before or after she is **racing** for seriously hindering a yacht which is **racing**, or for infringing the sailing instructions.

The definitions tell us that racing begins when the preparatory signal is given, and ends for a particular boat when she has cleared the finish line. Contact between boats is not necessary for a rule infringement to occur. Before or after a race a boat may do something to result in her penalization; but if it involves another boat, the other boat must have been "*seriously* hindered" (italics added). The "hindering" need not be a Part IV rule violation. For example, a starboard-tack boat could interfere with a port-tack boat. Interfering with another boat might be considered serious if as a result she obviously lost her position in the race. This might happen when a boat already finished takes the wind of a boat about to finish in a neck-and-neck race with a competitor. It might even happen if a distracting hail is given by a nonracer at a critical time. The onus would be on the hindered boat, however, to show that the hindrance was really "serious."

Sometimes the sailing instructions require boats to remain clear of a prescribed starting area until their preparatory signal has been sounded, and rule 31.2 would allow a boat violating this restriction to be penalized, even though her entry into the restricted area did not hinder a boat that was racing. Other examples include failure to wear a life jacket at the signal, and failure to sign a declaration after a race.

Throughout the rules of Part IV there are places where "disqualification" or "retirement" is mentioned, and these should always be taken to mean "disqualification or other prescribed penalty" and "retirement or other acknowledgment of an infringement" when the rules in use provide for lesser penalties than disqualification. This applies to rule 31.2, as well as to 32 (in referring to the non right-of-way boat), 33, 35.1, 43.3(b), and 43.3(c). Rule 46.3 is worded accurately. Unlike these, rule 32 probably means what it says, with reference to disqualification, because most penalty systems not otherwise using disqualification nevertheless do prescribe it when serious damage results.

Rule 32, which says, "A right-of-way yacht which fails to make a reasonable attempt to avoid a collision resulting in serious damage may be disqualified as well as the other yacht," uses two vague words in mentioning a "reasonable" attempt and "serious" damage. In any case, her attempt must not be perfunctory, nor made long after it might have been effective when there was time to take avoiding action earlier. Note that the damage need not be to the non right-of-way boat; it may be to both boats, or only to the right-of-way boat. The jury may disqualify or it may not—the rule's inclusion of the permissive word "may" suggests that it use its discretion.

In IYRU 53 (originally NAYRU 140), two Ps approached a windward mark with PL slightly ahead. PL tacked in front of PW, and was struck and seriously damaged by PW. PL was disqualified for violating 41.2, although the appeals committee did not disqualify PW under 32. The protest committee had disqualified PW under rule 49, "Fair Sailing." The appeals committee held PW blameless, even though she evidently made no attempt to avoid the collision, because once PL tacked she had barely time to do anything at all, and rule 32 does not require disqualification "automatically." Here is another example of the principle at work which says that a boat must be allowed time to respond to any obligation that is thrust suddenly upon her. In this case, this obligation was to make a reasonable attempt to avoid a collision.

Rule 33 says:

> A yacht which realizes she has infringed a racing rule or sailing instruction is under an obligation to retire promptly; but, when she persists in **racing**, other yachts shall continue to accord her such rights as she may have under the rules of Part IV.

The moralistic tone of this sentence says little more than that the rules should be followed, but it points up that a contestant may not be so sure as those around him that he has infringed a rule. Until he decides this, and either withdraws or acknowledges a penalty obligation in the way prescribed by such rules as the 720-degree Turns or Percentage Penalty systems stipulate, he is very much in the race. This means that such a boat may successfully protest another, even though the first boat is found guilty of an earlier infringement herself.

Rule 67: A Special Rule

Although not a rule of Part IV, rule 67 might have been included in Section A of Part IV rather than being placed where it is, in Part VI:

1. When there is contact between the hull, spars, standing rigging or crew of two yachts while racing, both shall be disqualified, unless one of them retires in acknowledgment of an infringement of the rules, or one or both of them acts in accordance with rule 68.3, Protests.

2. A third yacht which witnesses an apparent collision between two yachts, and, after finishing or retiring, discovers that neither of them has observed rule 67.1, is relieved by Rule 68.3(b) from the requirement of showing a protest flag and may lodge a protest against them.
3. The race committee may waive this rule when it is satisfied that minor contact was unavoidable.

The effect of rule 67 is to make it quite risky for either party in a boat-to-boat contact incident to ignore it. If neither retires, each should protest unless he is confident that the contact point on at least one boat was a sail or part of the running rigging(sheets or halyards), or that the protest committee will almost surely decide that the contact was "minor" *and* unavoidable. Otherwise both boats will be disqualified without regard to the rules that applied between them during the incident itself. Even if a modified penalty system is in use, unless the sailing instructions prescribe otherwise, the system will probably apply only to Part IV infractions. Thus, it can happen that you were fouled by another boat, chose not to protest, and were later disqualified (not merely penalized) because you did not protest. This action can occur as a result of a third-party protest or the race committee itself may call a hearing under its authority in rule 73.2. Or, although the third-party protest is filed under a Part IV rule, the protest committee can disqualify the innocent party also, under rule 67! Your best policy is to fly a flag after any boat-to-boat contact. You always have the option of retiring yourself, or deciding later not to file a written protest. The latter option is not available if you fail to fly your protest flag "at the first reasonable opportunity."

5

The Race: Rules and Tactics

Tactics must recognize all those considerations that determine the relative advantages or disadvantages a boat enjoys or suffers, as a result of its position in relation to nearby boats. A tactical move, therefore, is one that should be designed to exploit a favorable position or to defend against an unfavorable position. It can be offensive or defensive. A position can be favorable or unfavorable, as between two boats, if the wind is deflected by one against the other, or blocked off. The wake of a boat ahead is a natural barrier to her pursuer in some situations; in others it can be exploited by the boat behind. Third-party boats and other obstructions can sometimes be tactically exploited to advantage. And, of course, the rules affect tactics.

Rules are important determinants of tactical action, because most of them state a direct or indirect advantage to one boat, and, by contrast, a disadvantage to another. "Approach the starting line on the starboard tack" is such well-known tactical advice that it rarely requires mention. It is a pure case of a rule-oriented principle; if the rules were written so that the port-tack boat had right-of-way, this particular tactical idea would collapse.

The written and unwritten onus provisions that we've seen also affect tactical judgments, because they indicate the risk involved in taking a chance. On the windward leg, a port-tack boat risks being penalized if she attempts to cross ahead of a starboard tacker, even with what she may think is plenty of room. The appeals make it clear that in a hearing, the starboard-boat's claim that she had to fall off, or tack, will nearly always be accepted as the truth, while the other's assertion that this was not so will generally fall upon deaf ears.

There is also an item of racing *strategy* to keep in mind: it rarely pays to touch another boat. The exception is when you are encountering a confirmed rule-breaker who never withdraws and you are absolutely certain that the rules are wholly on your side. Otherwise, bear in mind that if there is boat-to-boat contact, a jury must penalize someone (with one exception), while if there is no contact the jury may find from the facts that no one infringed a rule. (The exception is in Rule 67; a jury may decide not to penalize two boats that contacted following a protest by a third party under this rule, if it finds that "minor" contact was unavoidable.)

To look at rules-based tactics in action, we will sail an imaginary race, around an Olympic course—a triangle, followed by a second windward leg, a run, and a final windward leg.

Before the Start

Before, during, and just after the start the water space taken up by boats may often seen excessive. Also, before the start, when there is no particular direction to go while at the same time everyone wants to be somewhere near the line, boat-to-boat encounters are both numerous and frequent. Here, your rules knowledge must be instinctive, because there is simply not enough time to think much about them.

Plan your start to cross the line on starboard tack, except in very special circumstances, such as an uncrowded line which favors the port end. The port tacker risks penalization if an S says he had to give way (rule 36 and the weight of appeals) and since P must keep clear of all S's he may need to delay his own start until he has passed astern of the entire fleet. There may sometimes be an advantage to starting on port even with this risk, if the starboard side of the windward leg is clearly the place to be. Passing astern of others usually means building up good speed, which is a gain over the others if most of them are backwinded by others in a crowd. But, by and large, start on starboard.

Getting onto starboard tack means either approaching from a long distance out, which is to be avoided if the wind is at all unstable, or coming from the port end of the line and then tacking. The latter is somewhat more difficult but is the method preferred by many top-rank skippers, because they can see what most of the opposition are doing and can select a point of entry in the oncoming group at any time up to very near the starting gun. They are not hindered by rule 34, not being right-of-way boats, so their maneuvers can be abrupt. However, while in the process of tacking they must heed 41.1 and 41.2 by being sure they complete their tack far enough from the starboard tackers to allow them to keep clear as required

The Race: Rules and Tactics — 115

by either 37.1 or 37.2. These require windward boats or boats astern to keep clear.

Once everyone is on the starboard tack and only a minute or less remains, boats will jockey for position by speeding up or slowing down and by moving down the line by sailing over or behind others, or by trying to hold position by pinching hard. Several rules define possible choices.

The boat moving down the line to windward of the others must keep clear of all of them, because they are leeward boats, with before-the-start rule-40 luffing rights. If she moves quickly and finds a hole to bear off into somewhere down the line, then she is safe. She must avoid a relatively new risk, however; the "one-minute" rule (51.1(c)) is in effect after a recalled start, and at many regattas is being placed in effect on the first start as well. It requires a boat over the line anytime during the final minute to round one end of the line. Hence, a boat passing to windward of others must be confident that she is below the line, or else near enough to one end of the line that she can round the mark without great loss of time.

A boat trying to hold her position by stalling has a fair amount of rules protection. She has no rules worries about windward boats, because they must stay clear of her (rule 37.1). Boats to leeward or behind and to leeward may cause problems; however, defense is possible. Rules 37.2, 37.3, 37.1, and 40 apply, in that order. The boat astern must keep clear before establishing an overlap (rule 37.2), whether or not the boat ahead is moving forward, standing still, or actually moving backward. The rule does not mention overtaking and overtaken boats, but rather boats ahead and astern. This is what gives a backward-moving boat that is ahead protection under 37.2. If you have luffed as high as a head-to-wind position from the starboard tack you retain your rights under rules 37.1, 37.2, 37.3, 40 (and 36), because you are still on a tack, as defined in Part I, "Definitions."

Rule 37.3 applies when the boat astern of you first establishes an overlap. If she is close you should consider luffing sharply to force her to leeward. If she fails to respond she has infringed 37.3 by failing to leave you enough room to keep clear. If you let the moment pass and she is close enough to touch you, you have lost 37.3's protection and are vulnerable under 37.1 or 40 or both.

Rule 40 is a dangerous weapon in the hands of a leeward boat that has come from astern of you. Once the brief protection period offered by 37.3 has come and gone, 40 allows your opponent to luff. If he is close to begin with, you will have serious difficulty in staying clear; since he is probably still not yet abeam of you, his bow and your stern will be alongside. To move your stern upwind your bow must go down, and this only makes matters worse. Be prepared to luff as soon as the overlap begins, or else to let the other boat move quickly into a position abeam or ahead of abeam. Only when your centerboard or keel is even with or aft of his will you be able to keep clear by luffing. As he gains the "mast abeam" position he also gains the right to luff head-to-wind rather than only up to a close-hauled position, but this is a safer condition for you when compared with the earlier one. Remember that you have rule 38.3 to help you; if the leeward boat is luffing above close-hauled before moving ahead of "mast abeam," hail "Mast abeam!" She must be governed by your hail during all stages of rule 40's applicability. The purpose of rule 38.3 is to give windward boats the right to limit a leeward-boat's luff by a hail that binds the leeward boat.

When starting near the starboard end of the line pay no heed to boats to windward of you who want to pass between you and the RC boat or buoy; under rule 42.3 the windward boat can expect no room. After the starting signal you must

The Race: Rules and Tactics – 117

fall off to close-hauled if otherwise you would deprive a W of room to pass the mark, but not otherwise. As a W in such circumstances, be especially cautious in starting close to the starboard end mark. There is no rule against it *per se* but, as we have just seen, a windward boat is extremely vulnerable. A slight clockwise wind shift can reduce or even eliminate any space you had, by allowing boats to leeward to sail closer to the RC boat.

Another hazardous spot exists when the RC uses a boat for the port end mark. Don't be tempted to start too close; the bow and anchor line of the RC boat must be cleared after you cross the line, and as a result a part of the line is rendered useless for starting:

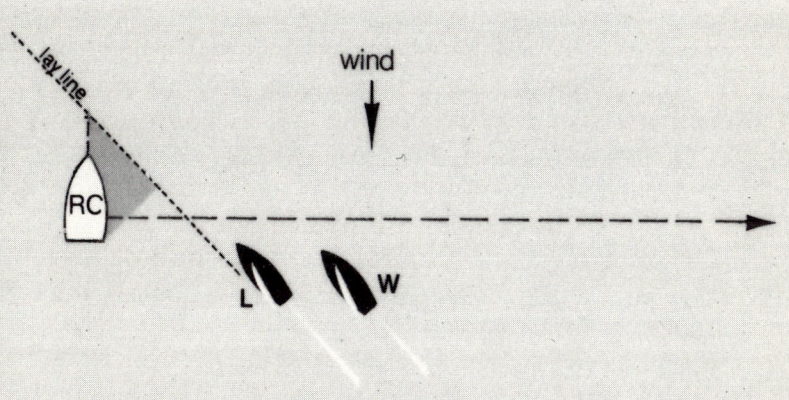

This is a "coffin corner" situation. If you get into it, and then must tack to avoid hitting the obstruction, rule 43.3 helps you from a safety viewpoint, but if a W who has been able to fetch the anchor line tacks out of your way, you are penalized (Rule 43.3(b)).

Remember that special luffing rights change as rule 38

supercedes 40; this is when the leeward boat has cleared the line. As either a W or an L, be aware of whether there was "mast abeam" at the time the leading boat's bow crossed the line (38.2); that determines L's luffing rights under 38.1 once she has cleared the line. As an L, you probably will not find it advantageous to spend time luffing a W when it is important for you to be going fast to escape the blanketing and backwind of others. However, there may be an occasion when a shout and a quick luff will be needed to ward off an overtaking W.

The Windward Leg

Tactical encounters when beating to windward usually arise when opposite-tack boats cross paths or are sailing close aboard one another on the same tack. Blanketing and backwinding are both formidable tactical weapons based on the use of wind. The rules can have a critical influence on how effectively these weapons can be used.

In a crossing situation, when you are S, remember the limitations imposed on you by rule 34. Being on starboard does not give you license to luff in close quarters when a P is crossing ahead of you. If you want P to tack in front of you (so that you can tack and not have her with you), hail loudly. P's chances in a rule-36 hearing are so poor that if there is any doubt she will either tack or go astern of you. If she starts to go astern and you want to tack, be sure you do so early enough so that she is not required to make a larger course change than would have been necessary in the absence of your tack; this would be taken as evidence that you violated rule 34 by obstructing her.

If you prefer that P continue on port tack, consider hailing her that she has plenty of room to cross ahead, then let her cross. Bearing off when several boat lengths from her will also reassure her that she can cross. Don't hail her and later claim you were fouled under rule 36; her defense will be rule 49, "Fair Sailing."

As a P in these situations, be sure your decision to continue on port tack or to tack is based on your own strategy and not on whether it looks as though you can clear S or not. Generally your decision should not be affected by the loss of a boat length required to go astern of an S. The exception is right after the start, when falling astern of one S would also mean falling astern of several more; here, you should tack onto starboard and then watch for your first chance to work your way toward the other side of the course.

Sometimes you will want to try to establish a "safe-leeward" position against another boat by approaching her on the opposite tack, then tacking just ahead, or ahead and to leeward. Tacking directly to leeward does not work, because you lose speed during the tack and W will blanket you before you are up to speed again.

If you approach on port tack be sure that when you complete your tack (you are on the new close-hauled course) your opponent has time to avoid you, as required by rule 37.2 or 37.1. Rule 41.2 requires this, and 41.3 puts the onus on you to show that you did so. Hailing always helps; a "Hold your course" before tacking may avoid a nervous tack and a rule-36 protest by the other boat; a "Tack complete" at the time your new course is achieved will call to everyone's attention on both boats the amount of space between boats at that moment. The safest policy is to tack so that your new course is about a boat width to leeward of the other; even if you are this close there is still no ground for your opponent to claim he would have struck you from astern.

In this same situation, remember that as a leeward boat whose tack is completed before W gains "mast abeam," you have rule 38.1's luffing rights immediately. If the race is a two-boat fight, don't hesitate to use this weapon; it is one rule that exists to serve tactical purposes exclusively.

If you are S and approach intending to tack ahead or to leeward of P, watch out for rule 34. As you come closer, he knows he must avoid you as per rule 36. You will be somewhat ahead of him; otherwise your plan is a bad one in the first place. Therefore, he will either tack or plan to bear off below you. Your tack must not obstruct him. You may try hailing "Hold your course," but he has no obligation to do so. If you can make it sound inviting—appealing to the fact that he need not bear off—the hail may be worthwhile. In any event, your tactic is less likely to succeed when applied against a P. He has complete freedom of choice in deciding to tack or bear off, and rule 34 limits you. In the earlier case, S has the same choice of tacking or bearing off below P, but P is not vulnerable to rule 34 while changing course. Therefore, the maneuver is more appealing to P's approaching S's than the reverse.

Rule 37.1 gives basic protection to a leeward boat that is more close-winded than the windward boat; the latter must keep clear regardless of rule 38's "mast abeam" relationship. That rule refers only to luffing in any case; L is not luffing but nevertheless is entitled to sail her own close-hauled course. Rule 37.1 also protects boats on the windward leg from those on leeward legs—*if* the boats coming down are on the same tack. An S going to windward has both 36 and 37.1 on her side, but a P must give way to any S's that may be reaching or running toward her. Other things being equal, try to be on starboard when in heavy traffic.

At Weather Marks

Assuming a marks-to-port course, try to avoid coming in on port tack and tacking at the mark. Even with no other boats nearby, the process of tacking just before beginning a reach or run causes a speed sacrifice that continues to cost boat lengths because you have been unable to enter the new leg with maximum speed. Always begin an offwind leg at top speed—only then can you make full use of gusts that arrive just after rounding.

Another reason to approach on starboard is to be able to have right-of-way over Ps trying to find a spot in line. But avoid carrying this to such an extreme that you arrive at the lay line when a long distance from the mark. Try for a spot that is five–ten lengths from the mark, depending on wind speed and the speed of your type of boat. Then tack in front, or just to leeward and ahead of, any approaching S's.

At the mark, remember that rule 42.2(b) allows you to claim room from anyone who has crossed ahead, then tacked to windward of you inside the circle, even though you gain your overlap on him afterward. Rule 37.1 is also on your side. If you approach on port, try to go on past the starboard-tack lay line to clear air, so that your tack can be made under good conditions.

Before and during the rounding, note whether there are any rule-38 luffing rights between you and overlapped boats. If you are L and have these rights you may want to sail high of your proper course while preparing to set a chute. If you are W and want to keep L from holding you high, hail "Mast abeam" as soon as you have it—even if this is before making the rounding. As long as that overlap continues, L may not luff above her proper course on the new leg.

Remember to look for boats still on the windward leg, especially if your new course is a run. On starboard, you must give 37.1 rights to those coming upwind on starboard. If they are on port, you can easily violate rule 34 if, in the process of bearing off to your new course too close to one of them, you make her alter course when she otherwise would have kept clear. Apart from this, your starboard tack gives you freedom to choose your course without restraint.

The Reach

Almost by definition, this is a leg on which everyone will sail on the same tack until just before rounding the "jibing" mark. The same-tack rules, 37, 38, 39, and their related definitions, are the predominant rule influences on tactics. The major wind influence, tactically, is blanketing, while bow and stern waves also have their effects. Your basic objective is to pass boats and to end the leg inside at the mark. On the first reach of a triangular course this means being to leeward; on the second it is the windward boat that finishes inside at the mark.

As said earlier, generally it does not pay to use rule 38.1's luffing rights, because the time lost is costly to both boats. The best way to discourage boats from passing to windward is to sail high briefly at the beginning of the leg. Also, if you have the speed, pass boats to windward by being sure you are well to windward of their courses before closing in. That way, the boat being overtaken will find that it is too late and too far to go, to luff up to your course.

By and large, then, boat-to-boat encounters should be few and the rules therefore usually do not offer important tactical opportunities, either offensive or defensive. However, as an L it will pay you to remember that neither rule 37.3 nor 38.1

prohibits you from luffing after W has gained "mast abeam"; they only prohibit you from sailing above your proper course. In most modern boats, the fastest course to the next mark will not be a straight line and on puffy days it will be especially important to bear off sharply in the gusts and luff in the lulls. Rule 37.1 allows the latter. Rule 35 implies that you should hail a W that may not see you coming up, and this is good tactical policy anyhow. Hail "Proper course" so that she is less likely to hail "Mast abeam." Rule 38.3 allows her to stop you with such a hail even when she is not entitled to do so. You would have to protest to prove that you were entitled to luff because your "proper course" allowed it.

As a W, be wary of rule 39 but not unnecessarily so. You may steer below your proper course if the boat behind is not "steering a course to pass to leeward" of you. If your proper course takes you right down close abeam of a boat overlapped to leeward you may bear off, as long as you continue to keep clear of her as rule 37.1 requires. Toward the end of the leg your proper course is to be close to the mark, so feel free to position yourself in front of a boat astern sailing a more leeward course.

At the Jibing Mark

Sometimes the second mark of the Olympic course is called the jibing mark, although a jibe is also often made at the following mark when it is being used later at the end of the run. The course from starboard-tack reach to port-tack reach inevitably calls for a jibe, however, and rules 37, 38, and 42.1(a)(i) and (ii) govern the tactics of overlapped boats.

The inside boat can claim room to round, and is also protected as the leeward boat by rule 37.1. If she has rule 38.1 rights, she may apply team or match-race tactics and keep W from bearing off or jibing by holding her course. Rule 38.1 allows her to sail above her proper course. However, if W has obtained "mast abeam" earlier, L must bear off and jibe "in order most directly" to assume her proper course to the next mark.

If W is somewhat behind L, she should consider slowing down deliberately, then luffing across the other's stern after the jibe, to be able to gain clear air and the possibility of passing to windward. L, on her part, should jibe smoothly but close to the mark, ready to discourage the other boat by a brief luff.

If L was behind on arriving at the mark she should avoid being pressured into a too-sharp rounding by the outside boat. (Refer to the discussion of "room" on page 69.) If L turns sharply she slows too much and allows the outside boat to gain clear air by moving ahead. The tactic for the outsider is to avoid allowing more room than is required, by making her turn just as smoothly as possible to avoid loss of momentum. After her jibe she may or may not have rule 38.1 rights, but she does have 37.1 rights, and if she needs to luff to a higher course to regain speed, the "proper course" concept allows her to do so.

The Leeward Mark—From the Reach

At this mark the fleet will be rounding with windward boats inside, and luffing to a close-hauled course rather than jibing. Otherwise there is little difference, and the applicable rules are generally the same—37, 38, and 42. When entering the two-length circle, try to luff out ahead of boats to windward and behind, and then bear off sharply to break the overlap before entering the circle. In cases where the real battle is between you and the boat astern—as may happen in the final race of a series with a throw-out race—remember rule 42.1(a)(iv). With rule 38.1 luffing rights you can hail and then take your opponent to the wrong side of the mark, if you go along. Sail high enough so that when she tacks to return you have the choice of jibing to return. On the way back, as leeward boat you can prevent her from bearing off to round if she has not gained "mast abeam" on the new tack. If she has gained it, you must sail no higher than your proper course (to the mark, in this situation), and thereafter must jibe. As inside boat, however, you should win.

If you are W, be alert to L's hail and luff. Sail only as high as she forces you to, and if you are clever and can slow down to the point where her bow is just beyond the mark at the moment you have let her pull ahead of you, you may be able to bear off sharply and round the mark. For this to work, the other boat will have made the mistake of passing too close to windward of the mark.

An outside boat during the approach should try to work ahead enough to be able to break an overlap just before reaching the circle, by bearing off and hailing loudly as she does so (see rule 35.2). If the overlap existed until this stage, the onus will be hers (rule 42.2(e)(ii)) to convince the committee that she broke it in time. There is no particular defense for the inside boat; neither luffing nor bearing off is likely to help her keep the overlap. She should be ready to hail (at the right time) that the overlap remains, even though her hail is not specifically listed in rule 35 as a means of strengthening her case.

If the positions are reversed and the inside boat is ahead she should demand enough room to round "in safety" and avoid any abrupt rudder movements that will slow her unnecessarily. The outside boat has rule 37.1 on her side, which still applies even though modified by 42.1(a)(i). She need not delay luffing up to her close-hauled course at the end of the rounding maneuver, and if the insider fails to make a seamanlike rounding, reasonably close to the mark, she is nevertheless obligated to stay clear of the outsider, L.

The Run

A run is any course that involves sailing on each tack for some part of the time, assuming that one is sailing at optimum speed and angle to the true wind. The ideal run is with the course directly parallel to the wind direction, but in practice ideal runs are infrequent and one tack is therefore favored.

As on windward legs, Ps and S's converge and rule 36 applies. Because varying wind velocity, as well as direction, determines a boat's best course, there is greater chance on the run for a foul under either rule 36 or 34. A P may find that her plan to cross ahead of an S fails when on a light day S gets an accelerating puff. Also, S may luff or bear off in adjusting to a different wind strength and P will need to jibe or luff up astern of S. Unless the two boats are so close together that rule 34 prevents S from changing course, S has complete freedom of movement.

If either S or P jibes, rule 41 applies. Be sure you allow more space for your jibe than for a tack; a well-executed jibe requires a turning circle of much greater radius. Catamarans in particular must be jibed without sharp turns. Your jibe is complete when your sail is "filled" and this can be argued to mean when the wind first pushes it across rather than when the boom stops moving. However, most committees probably take the latter view.

During the run, give plenty of room to same-tack boats or starboard tackers beating to windward. On a windy day with chute set you are less able to change course in a hurry if a shift causes the oncoming boat to change hers. You have rule 34 on your side if the two boats are close to each other, but since you are approaching each other almost head-on, the distance disappears quickly and the committee may decide that you simply did not respond in time to your rule 37.1 or 36 obligations.

When overlapped with a same-tack boat, remember that you can regain lost luffing rights by widening out beyond two boat lengths, or by jibing twice, as long as you are ahead of "mast abeam" when finished.

The Leeward Mark—From the Run

Approaching this mark, the fleet will be coming from a variety of directions and on either tack, and the definition of overlap and rule 42 combine to cover most boat-to-boat encounters. Remember that an overlap depends on whether one boat is clear astern of another, and that this in turn depends on an imaginary line projected perpendicularly from the "aftermost point of the other's hull and equipment."

If you are the outside of two boats sailing essentially parallel courses, in danger of being overlapped by an insider just astern, do not alter course to windward until you have entered the two-length circle. Only a slight luff will swing the perpendicular line aft on your windward side, and you will have made a gift of the overlap to your opponent.

If you are inside, on the other hand, keep a watch on boats approaching from a wide angle to your course; more often than not you will have an overlap on them before they enter the circle. True, they may be going fast enough to round the mark before you arrive, but if you arrive at about the same time be sure to hail for room (35.2 again) when still outside the circle.

If you approach on starboard tack and delay your jibe until during the rounding, remember that "room includes room . . . to . . . jibe" when that is part of the rounding maneuver. Your jibe must be "seamanlike" but by no means perfect, and the outsider must allow room for the swing of your boom as well as the normal amount of hull room. As before, when rounding this mark from the second reach, rules 37.1 and 42.1(a)(i) both apply, and once past the mark the windward insider must stay clear.

At the Finish

Good committees set rather short finish lines so as to minimize any advantage from one end of the line being more to leeward than the other, and also to be better able to record sail numbers. Usually traffic is light but sometimes a jam occurs.

Finish marks, including a race-committee boat, are treated the same under the rules as other marks of the course except for starting marks. Rule 42 allows an inside overlapped boat to call for room. Also, since the committee boat is also an obstruction, unless it is unusually small and the boats are unusually large, the leeward of two close-hauled boats approaching on port tack can hail the windward boat about under rule 43, unless of course the latter can clear the windward end of the committee boat and its anchor line.

Finish-line tactics are little different from windward-leg tactics except for rule-42 considerations. If you have overstood slightly and are on a converging course with an overlapped boat to leeward, assert your rights to room with a loud hail. However, don't foul L by bearing off too soon before the two-length circle protects you.

6

When You Go to Court

There are no courts in yacht racing but the sport's penalty system, which includes formal notification, written accusation, hearing, and possible appeal is so analogous to society's legal system that the basic ideas behind both are the same. In this regard, sailing is quite unlike other sports in which infringements are observed and the rules enforced by umpires or referees on the spot. In sailing, officials may observe infractions but they may not impose a penalty without a hearing, with the exception of boats failing to start or finish. The penalty system relies almost exclusively on the contestants themselves acknowledging their own infringements and accepting the penalty; or, when an opponent fails to do so, bringing the matter before a protest committee or jury for a hearing and subsequent decision. Therefore, any serious competitor should know the main elements of the full procedure, and especially his rights as either protestor or protestee.

Do not deceive yourself that sailing's legal system is any nearer perfection than others. A realistic view of how protest committees and juries function on all levels from local club racing to major international regattas shows that, with the best of intentions, committees often make mistakes. The number of appeals that overturn lower-level decisions confirms this, and there must be many other cases that are not brought to appeal.

The point is this: stay out of trouble; avoid contact with other boats even if you are convinced at the time that you are in the right. Later, a committee may decide otherwise. Also, if you have a grievance but there was no contact, be sure of your case before taking it to a hearing. The decision may go against you, and even if there was no contact, you may be penalized for an infringement.

On the other hand, if after an altercation you feel strongly that you have been wronged, prepare your case with care, argue it to the best of your ability, and be willing to appeal if, after the decision is made, you think it is wrong. This is what racing's legal system is there for—to determine accurately rights and wrongs between contestants. The more the appeal procedure is used the better will be the quality of jury work at regattas.

This chapter concentrates on the penalty system as it applies to Part IV infractions, but Part VI of the rulebook, "Protests, Disqualifications and Appeals," covers other matters the reader will want to examine for himself. The rules of Part VI that deal with the means of enforcing other rules are actually longer than the right-of-way rules of Part IV. They need not be studied quite so thoroughly, but the main details are important. They prescribe everything that can or should happen, beginning immediately after the incident in question and ending with the decision of the final appeals authority. Let's consider developments as they happen.

On the Water

You and another boat have just had an "altercation," an "incident," or whatever you choose to call it. There may or may not have been contact between you, but one or both feels strongly that the other has infringed a Part-IV rule. Later, during the race or on shore, one or both of you may decide to retire or otherwise acknowledge your rule infraction, and the process will end there. The race committee will record the admission and adjust the score accordingly. However, these are possible future events; what about the time just after the incident?

First, look around to see what other boats were nearby and, if possible, write down their numbers. If that is impractical, say them aloud within your crew; if there are more than two or three, assign each crew member to remember particular numbers. At the same time, all of you should try to remember the general position of these boats. You want these numbers so that you can ask their skippers and crews to be witnesses at the hearing.

Next, fly your protest flag as soon as you have your boat organized and moving again. This assumes you have a flag aboard. You should, if only for the unlikely eventuality that someday you will be seriously damaged by a competitor who may not want to pay for the repairs. A formal protest and hearing, on record, will help you pursue the financial claim. To play safe, be sure your flag is as prescribed in the sailing instructions. Rule 68.3 says Code Flag "B" is acceptable "irrespective" of what the sailing instructions say, but rule 3.1 allows the sailing instructions to change rule 68.3 if they refer specifically to it.

The reason you should fly your flag is to keep open your option to protest. Later on, you may decide you were in the wrong, or that no rule was broken by either party. Or, you may decide for any number of reasons that you prefer not to pursue the matter. (Some of these reasons may be legitimate, while others are not; sailors' opinions differ.) You need not submit a protest, and if you choose not to do so you need not feel obliged to apologize for flying the flag in the first place. You should fly it in order to have time to think.

Rule 68.3(a) requires that the flag be flown "at the first reasonable opportunity." Reasonableness can be interpreted loosely, and appeals committees generally take the view that a protest should be heard unless it is quite clear that a flag was not flown in reasonable time. In RYA 64/26, the flag went up some fifty minutes after an incident between two three-man keelboats, in winds of less than ten knots. The boats were on a weather leg, and the protesting skipper convinced the committee that the undivided attention of all three crew members was necessary for controlling the mainsheet, jibsheet, and tiller! Most committees will not accept a fifty-minute delay on such grounds, and your best policy will be to fly your flag as soon as possible, without unduly sacrificing your boat-handling.

At the same time or before, hail your adversary "Protesting, number —." This starts him thinking about whether he should retire, and also protects you from another technicality later. Your protest will not be heard unless you meet rule 68.3(c)'s requirement that you "shall try" to inform the other boat that you will protest. Note that you need not *succeed* in informing him; if he claims he did not hear your hail the protest will nonetheless be heard.

If as you approach the finish your flag is still up, hail the committee after you cross that you are protesting boat number such-and-such. This is not required (although sailing instructions sometimes require it), but it alerts the committee that it should expect a written protest. It can save you valuable time at the end of the day also, by alerting the committee chairman to the need for scheduling a hearing and notifying other committee members of its time and place.

On Shore

As soon as possible after the race, obtain a protest form if they are prescribed, line up your witnesses, find out when and where the protest must be filed, and sit down with your crew, and perhaps a friend whose rules knowledge you respect, to discuss the incident and the applicable rules. At regattas a quiet place is difficult to find, but sitting in a car somewhere down the street is much preferable to the club bar or other place where people are constantly coming and going.

The purpose of this meeting is to talk over the details of what happened so that your protest will be written clearly, and to plan your presentation. In this regard it may help you to ask the chairman of the jury or protest committee how he normally proceeds in conducting a hearing. Ask him if the two parties can cross-examine each other; if you can ask the witnesses questions yourself; and if you can present a short summary of your position at the end. An experienced chairman will plan to use all of these procedures, and an inexperienced chairman will probably take notice of your questions and realize that he should find out what the recommended procedure is. Your rules-expert friend can be very helpful at this stage, because by telling him what happened, you will be rehearsing your testimony, and he can also help evaluate your judgments as to how the rules apply. In planning your testimony, make notes of the main points you want to make, and which witnesses can comment on each point.

The written protest must include details of date, time, race, location, wind and water conditions, etc., and these are called for automatically on standard protest forms. If no form is available, read rule 68.3(d). The heart of the protest is a description of what happened, regardless of what form is used. Your statement about what rules apply can help by impressing the committee with your understanding of the rules, but rule 72.1 makes it clear that you need not refer to the correct rule in order in win your case. Try to write what happened in a step-by-step sequence, and refer to a diagram if that helps your explanation.

Next, be sure you hand in the protest on time, and to a member of the protest committee or jury, preferably its chairman. If something keeps you from meeting the deadline, by all means hand in the protest anyhow, and if there is an objection ask for a hearing to explain your delay. The committee has authority to extend the filing deadline (rule 68.3(e)(i)) but must have some reason beyond an arbitrary decision to do so. NAYRU 88 confirms this.

The Hearing

Once a written protest is filed a hearing must be held (rule 68.6) unless all questions are settled by one or more boats retiring. The hearing must be held "as soon as possible" (rule 70), although if it is not, there is no recourse available against the committee. The committee can refuse to hear a protest only if it informs you of its reasons, and must allow you a hearing to show that you did meet all requirements for a hearing (rule 69). Although rule 73 allows a disqualification without protest if a boat fails to start or finish, the committee must allow a hearing if the skipper convinces it "that an error *may* have been made" (italics added). Most scoring systems, including the Olympic, provide for "DNS" or "DNF" rather than disqualification, and although the rules do not mention it specifically a race committee will in all likelihood allow anyone a hearing who believes that he was recorded DNS or DNF erroneously. The purpose of all these various provisions is to prevent technicalities from standing in the way of a fair settlement of any legitimate rules question.

A proper hearing will follow the procedure recommended by the IYRU, described in its Yearbook and, in shorter form, in the NAYRU rulebook. It calls for a reading of the protest and any other written submissions by either party, a statement of the facts and applicable rules as seen by the protester, the protestee's statement of facts and rules, questions by all parties of the other parties, statements by witnesses and questions by any party, and of course questions by members of the protest committee or jury of any of the parties or witnesses. Each party may be present at all times; everyone else may be excluded excepting witnesses when testifying (rule 70). There is no requirement that anyone be excluded, and committees that allow observers, as long as order is maintained, probably help the sport by encouraging better understanding of rules and procedure.

You may want to consider having someone else present your protest; the rule does not require that you be your own "representative." Your crew or a friend may know the rules better; he also may be able to help your case by casting you in the role of witness during the hearing. Probably most committees will feel they are in the presence of a "big city lawyer" if you use this approach, but it may be worth considering in special circumstances. Even protest hearings have their strategic considerations.

The committee is required to "take the evidence presented by the parties" (rule 70) and you should be allowed to present it in your own way, both in your initial presentation and in putting questions to your witnesses. However, avoid annoying the committee by dragging matters out unnecessarily. In fact, avoid annoying them in any way. Being human, they may be biased against you and, as a result, their decision may reflect this.

Your approach to the committee and your opponent should be polite and as calm in demeanor as you can manage. This is one more reason for asking for ample time to prepare; tempers can cool if the hearing is delayed for a reasonable length of time. In the hearing you may have to educate the committee about the meaning of rules and significance of appeals; if so, be as tactful as possible. Needless to say, you may find that the committee will improve your understanding of the rules too.

Be careful not to interrupt others in their testimony, or to argue when it is not your turn to speak. Make notes of what others say when you want to rebut their statements later. For the same reason, do not be afraid to say "Please let me finish" when you are interrupted, even by a committee member, when the interruption seriously hinders your presentation.

In describing what happened, try to include your estimates of distances between boats, or seconds elapsed between events, or both. Often such details can make all the difference—rule 41.2 is an example—and when you present these details confidently and with support from your crew and other witnesses, your case is more solid. Often you can add supporting detail, such as, "My crew was already out on the trapeze when the other boat hit our transom. This shows that we had completed our tack some seconds before."

If you are the protestee you should follow many of the same steps that a protester should take. Talk the incident over with your crew, witnesses, and a noninvolved friend who knows the rules. Ask to see the written protest as soon as it is available, and for a copy, if this is possible. Read it carefully and then decide how much time you require to prepare your defense. Few people do this; the rules require that you be allowed adequate time (rule 70). If you are late getting to the hearing and find that a decision has already been made, protest this vigorously and in writing; rule 70.3 allows a decision in your absence only if you fail to make "an effort" to attend the hearing. If you were not informed of the time and place accurately, or were delayed unavoidably, you must be granted a hearing (see NAYRU 104). If it happens that you were not protested but are called into a hearing because testimony of others has indicated that you may be at fault in an incident, you have all rights of a protestee including availability of the protest, time to prepare a defense, and being present during all statements by others. This means that the hearing may be delayed, and in any case previous testimony will have to be repeated. Nonetheless, these are important rights and you should not willingly give them up. Rule 72.1 says you can be penalized even though you were not named in the original protest.

"Interested parties" may not take part in the discussion leading to a decision or the decision itself, and this means that no contestant may be a member of the protest committee or jury (NAYRU 124). Since an interested party is "anyone who stands to gain or lose" from the decision (rule 75), this probably means that no member of a sailor's immediate family should be on the committee, inasmuch as they have a strong personal interest.

Also, when a hearing is being held as the result of a sailor "seeking redress" from the race committee because it has, in his view, hurt his chances by some act or failure to act (rule 68.5(a)), the committee holding the hearing should not include members of the race committee who conducted the race. Race committee members are not interested parties in the sense that they stand to gain or lose points in the regatta scoring, obviously, but their reputation stands to suffer if they make a serious error in race management. If unbiased judgment is what the rules are protecting when they exclude interested parties, then race-committee members in such circumstances are inappropriate members of the hearing committee. As a practical matter, the rules do not prohibit race committee members from deciding such cases, although some enlightened officials will arrange for rule 68.5 hearings to be held by others.

On the other hand, when the race committee has initiated the hearing in its role of umpire or referee (rule 73.2, somewhat misleadingly called "Disqualification without Protest"), one or more of its members may testify as witnesses—and must be subject to questions by the accused boat's representative, if he wishes—while remaining as a member of the decision-making committee (NAYRU 111 and RYA 63/1). Ideally, race committee members should never be protest committee or jury members, because even when the race committee accuses a boat of infringing the rules it thereby acquires an emotional interest in seeing that party found guilty. Until the rules of Part IV change, however, you had best tread lightly in a hearing called against you by the committee. You will not necessarily lose your case but you are "talking to the sheriff from inside the jail." Explain your case as best you can, with helpful witnesses, if you can find them.

There are times when you may have infringed a rule of

Part IV, and even freely admit this during a hearing, but will not be penalized. This should be the result when you have fouled because you were forced to do so by another boat. Rule 72.1(b) has been interpreted to allow the committee to absolve you from guilt, although the rule says only that a boat causing someone else to foul should be penalized. However, you must show that you had little or no way of avoiding the foul.

Several appeals bear on this use of rule 72.1(b). NAYRU 11 did *not* exonerate a leeward P when a windward P failed to respond to her hail under rule 43, resulting in an S being fouled. The appeals committee found that LP could have borne off below S. But in IYRU 6, originally RYA 62/37, in the same circumstances, PL was exonerated under 72.1(b). The appeals committee said that the rules did not require PL to foresee that PW would not respond, nor did they require her to bear off below S. This case contradicts the implication of NAYRU 11 that PL should go below S or otherwise be penalized, and as an IYRU case it should carry more weight.

NAYRU 71 exonerates a P who was struck by an S, and also exonerates S from violating rule 34 because she had been forced to do so by a different P. The appeals committee conceded that its authority to exonerate anyone rests only on an inferential interpretation of rule 72.1(b).

On the other side, RYA 63/22 disqualified four boats, all barging against a fifth, even though the original committee had exonerated one of the bargers because she had luffed into the boat nearest her in order to try to keep clear of the boat just to leeward. As a group the appeals are not always consistent, and this judgment would probably not have been made in North America. NAYRU 142 is the most recent of such cases, and indicates that rule 72.1(b) cannot always be used as a shield against being penalized for an "unavoidable" infringement. Two close-hauled Ps again approach a close-hauled S. PL sees the situation developing but does not hail PW until being hailed herself by S. She was not exonerated, because she waited too long to hail under rule 43. In all such circumstances the best policy is to assert your own rights early, and avoid collisions if there is time. You need not anticipate another's failure to give you the right-of-way, however, and can expect to be exonerated when you have been forced to foul.

After the Hearing

Once its decision is made, the committee will inform all parties. If you are unhappy with the results and believe you may want to appeal later, now is the time to ask for a written decision. Rule 71 says you must be given this, including any diagrams, *if* you ask. The decision will include the committee's version of the facts, and the applicable rules. Your appeal must go first to the next highest appeals body; this may be on the association level or on the highest level—your country's appeals body. If the appeal is decided in your favor it still may not change the results of the race in question. Unfortunately, rule 3.2 (b)(xvii) allows sailing instructions to rule out appeals for purposes of determining series results. But you will have the satisfaction of knowing you were right.

Rules 77 and 78 contain other information about the appeals procedure. A race committee may appeal if its decision has been overturned by an intermediate appeals committee. This is an interesting provision in that it allows the committee to act as though it were an interested party. IYRU rule 78.2 requires that when an appeal is made all parties be notified and invited to make comment on the appeal, although this rule has not been adopted explicitly by the

NAYRU. However, NAYRU rule 77.2(b) provides for notification and 78.8 implies that comments will be considered. Thus, if you find that an appeal has been filed that might overturn a decision that was favorable to you, ask for a copy of the appeal and then submit you own ideas about it. It is technically possible for a competitor not involved in the original hearing to file an appeal as an interested party, although there have been no appeals on the national level of this kind.

Your Rights: A Summary

Your "bill of rights" as a defendant include the following:

1. The right to see or have a copy of the protest (rule 70).
2. The right to be told the time and place of the hearing (rule 70).
3. The right to a "reasonable time" to prepare your defense (rule 70).
4. The right to state your case and call witnesses in support of it (rule 70).
5. The right to be present during your opponent's testimony and testimony of all witnesses (rule 70).
6. The right to receive a "prompt" decision, in writing and with the committee's diagram, if you ask (rule 71).
7. The right to submit an appeal (rule 77), except that the sailing instructions may prevent its use for changing the race results (rule 3.2(b)(xvii)).

As a protester, you have rights 2, 4, 5, 6, and 7 plus these:

8. The right to be informed of reasons for the committee's decision not to hear your protest and to have a hearing to

present evidence that you did comply with all requirements for submitting it (rule 69).
9. The right to remedy any defects in details in the original protest (rule 68.3(f)).
10. The right to pay any required deposit, after first being required to do so (rule 68.3(f)).

7

Maintaining Your Rules Knowledge

Books about the rules tend to be considerably longer than the rules themselves. If you have read this far you realize that a small detail, even a single word, may determine the outcome of a hearing. It is easy to forget the details of the rules, but there are some interesting ways to keep them fresh in mind. Here are some suggestions:

1. Join your National Authority—the North American Yacht Racing Union, the Canadian Yachting Association, the Royal Yachting Association, the Australian and New Zealand Yachting Federations are the major ones for English-speaking yachtsmen—and study its rulebook for any changes it may have made in the IYRU rules.

2. Read the appeals published by the National Authority, using this procedure: read the facts as found by the protest committee, then put the appeal aside and go to your rulebook. Pretend you are the committee and decide which rules apply and what boat, if any, should be penalized. Then read the appeal. If you disagree you probably will discover an error in your own thinking. On the other hand, not all the appeals are totally sound. You may discover something that the appeals committee missed. Consider also reading the IYRU cases, available from the NAYRU, CYA, or other national authorities.

3. At your own club and at regattas, look for hearing decisions posted on bulletin boards. Read them as you would an appeal, testing your rules knowledge against that of the protest committee or jury. It is good mental exercise and helps you stay rules-conscious.

4. Think about and discuss on-the-water incidents with others after the day's racing. You will hear opinions about the rules this way, and the discussion will sharpen your own thinking. Be prepared to change your mind about your own interpretation. The idea is not to hold a debate but to get at the meaning of the rules. Discuss the results of hearings with your friends, too.

5. Follow the sailing magazines. Most of them have frequent short articles about the rules and often a major article. If you disagree with a magazine writer's interpretation, write a letter to the editor. After the IYRU meetings in November of an Olympic Games year, look for articles describing the changes in the rules. Often these are written by members of the IYRU Rules Committee.

6. Read the various books on the rules. Each one offers something the others do not.

7. Offer to give a short talk on the rules to your club's

Maintaining Your Rules Knowledge – 145

junior-program members. You may find yourself in demand at other speaking occasions, if the word gets out that you do a good job. Giving such talks, with questions afterward from the audience, helps keep you prepared to answer rules questions quickly.

A conviction underlying this book is that the rules can be understood and remembered more easily if one sees the reasons behind them, how they relate to each other, and how "case law"—the appeals—has added to the rules as well as interpreting their meaning. Later editions will reflect changes in the rules and new interpretations. Meanwhile, if you have additions or changes to suggest, please write the author in care of the publisher: Dodd, Mead & Company, 79 Madison Avenue, New York, N.Y. 10016.

APPENDIX A

The 1973 Yacht Racing Rules of the International Yacht Racing Union, Parts I, IV, and VI

Note:

Marginal markings indicate the changes made in the text of the 1969 racing rules.

In translating and interpreting these rules, it shall be understood that the word "shall" is mandatory, and the words "can" and "may" are permissive.

Right of way when not subject to the racing rules

The rules of Part IV do not apply in any way to a vessel which is neither intending to race nor racing; such vessel shall be treated in accordance with the International Regulations for Preventing Collisions at Sea or Government Right-of-Way Rules applicable in the area concerned.

PART I—DEFINITIONS

When a term defined in Part I is used in its defined sense it is printed in **bold** *type. All definitions and italicized notes rank as rules.*

Racing—A yacht is **racing** from her preparatory signal until she has either **finished** and cleared the finishing line and finishing **marks** or retired, or until the race has been **cancelled, postponed** or **abandoned,** except that in match or team races, the sailing instructions may prescribe that a yacht is **racing** from any specified time before the preparatory signal.

Starting—A yacht **starts** when, after fulfilling her penalty obligations, if any, under rule 51.1(c), Sailing the Course, and after her starting signal, any part of her hull, crew or equipment first crosses the starting line in the direction of the course to the first **mark.**

Finishing—A yacht **finishes** when any part of her hull, or of her crew or equipment in normal position, crosses the finishing line from the direction of the course from the last **mark,** after fulfilling her penalty obligations, if any, under rule 52.2, Touching a Mark.

Luffing—Altering course towards the wind until head to wind.

Tacking—A yacht is **tacking** from the moment she is beyond head to wind until she has **borne away,** if beating to windward, to a **close-hauled** course; if not beating to windward, to the course on which her mainsail has filled.

Bearing Away—Altering course away from the wind until a yacht begins to **gybe.**

Gybing—A yacht begins to **gybe** at the moment when, with the wind aft, the foot of her mainsail crosses her centre line, and completes the **gybe** when the mainsail has filled on the other **tack.**

On a Tack—A yacht is **on a tack** except when she is **tacking** or **gybing.** A yacht is on the **tack (starboard** or **port)** corresponding to her **windward** side.

Close-hauled—A yacht is **close-hauled** when sailing by the wind as close as she can lie with advantage in working to windward.

Clear Astern and **Clear Ahead; Overlap**—A yacht is **clear astern** of another when her hull and equipment in normal position are abaft an imaginary line projected abeam from the aftermost point of the other's hull and equipment in normal position. The other yacht is **clear ahead.** The yachts **overlap** if neither is **clear astern;** or if, although one is **clear astern,** an intervening yacht **overlaps** both of them. The terms **clear astern, clear ahead** and **overlap** apply to yachts on opposite **tacks** only when they are subject to rule 42, Rounding or Passing Marks and Obstructions.

Leeward and **Windward**—The **leeward** side of a yacht is that on which she is, or, if **luffing** head to wind, was, carrying her mainsail. The opposite side is the **windward** side.

When neither of two yachts on the same **tack** is **clear astern,** the one on the **leeward** side of the other is the **leeward yacht.** The other is the **windward yacht.**

Proper course—A **proper course** is any course which a yacht might sail after the starting signal, in the absence of the other yacht or yachts affected, to **finish** as quickly as possible. The course sailed before **luffing** or **bearing away** is presumably, but not necessarily, that yacht's **proper course.** There is no **proper course** before the starting signal.

Mark—A **mark** is any object specified in the sailing instructions which a yacht must round or pass on a required side.

Every ordinary part of a **mark** ranks as part of it, including a flag, flagpole, boom or hoisted boat, but excluding ground tackle and any object either accidentally or temporarily attached to the **mark.**

Obstruction—An **obstruction** is any object, including craft under way, large enough to require a yacht, if not less than one overall length away from it, to make a substantial alternation of course to pass on one side or the other, or any object which can be passed on one side only, including a buoy when the yacht in question cannot safely pass between it and the shoal or object which it marks.

Cancellation—A **cancelled race** is one which the race committee decides will not be sailed thereafter.

Postponement—A **postponed** race is one which is not started at its scheduled time and which can be sailed at any time the race committee may decide.

Abandonment—An **abandoned** race is one which the race committee declares void at any time after the starting signal, and which can be re-sailed at its discretion.

PART IV—SAILING RULES WHEN YACHTS MEET

Helmsman's Rights and Obligations Concerning Right of Way

The rules of Part IV apply only between yachts which either are intending to **race** *or are* **racing** *in the same or different races, and, except when rule 3.2(b)(ii) applies, replace the International Regulations for Preventing Collisions at Sea or Government Right-of-Way Rules applicable to the area concerned, from the time a yacht intending to* **race** *begins to sail about in the vicinity of the starting line until she has either* **finished** *or retired and has left the vicinity of the course.*

SECTION A—RULES WHICH ALWAYS APPLY

31—Disqualification

1. A yacht may be disqualified or otherwise penalized for infringing a rule of Part IV only when the infringement occurs while she is **racing,** whether or not a collision results.

2. A yacht may be disqualified before or after she is **racing** for seriously hindering a yacht which is **racing,** or for infringing the sailing instructions.

32—Avoiding Collisions

A right-of-way yacht which fails to make a reasonable attempt to avoid a collision resulting in serious damage may be disqualified as well as the other yacht.

33—Retiring from Race

A yacht which realizes she has infringed a racing rule or a sailing instruction is under an obligation to retire promptly; but, when she persists in **racing,** other yachts shall continue to accord her such rights as she may have under the rules of Part IV.

34—Right-of-Way Yacht Altering Course

When one yacht is required to keep clear of another, the right-of-way yacht shall not so alter course as to prevent the other yacht from keeping clear, or so as to obstruct her while she is keeping clear, except:

(a) to the extent permitted by rule 38.1, Right-of-Way Yacht Luffing after Starting, and

(b) when assuming a **proper course** to **start,** unless subject to the second part of rule 44.1 (b), Yachts Returning to Start.

35—Hailing

1. Except when **luffing** under rule 38.1, Luffing after Starting, a right-of-way yacht which does not hail before or when making an alteration of course which may not be foreseen by the other yacht may be disqualified as well as the yacht required to keep clear when a collision resulting in serious damage occurs.

2. A yacht which hails when claiming the establishment or termination of an **overlap** or insufficiency of room at a **mark** or **obstruction** thereby helps to support her claim for the purposes of rule 42, Rounding or Passing Marks and Obstructions.

SECTION B—OPPOSITE TACK RULE

36—Fundamental Rule

A **port-tack** yacht shall keep clear of a **starboard-tack** yacht.

SECTION C—SAME TACK RULES

37—Fundamental Rules

1. A **windward yacht** shall keep clear of a **leeward yacht.**

2. A yacht **clear astern** shall keep clear of a yacht **clear ahead.**

3. A yacht which establishes an **overlap** to **leeward** from **clear astern** shall allow the **windward yacht** ample room and opportunity to keep clear, and during the existence of that **overlap** the **leeward yacht** shall not sail above her **proper course.**

38—Right-of-Way Yacht Luffing after Starting

1. **Luffing Rights and Limitations.** After she has **started** and cleared the starting line, a yacht **clear ahead** or a **leeward yacht** may **luff** as she pleases, except that:—

A **leeward yacht** shall not sail above her **proper course** while an **overlap** exists if, at any time during its existence, the helmsman of the **windward yacht** (when sighting abeam from his normal station and sailing no higher than the **leeward yacht**) has been abreast or forward of the mainmast of the **leeward yacht**.

2. **Overlap Limitations.** For the purpose of this rule: An **overlap** does not exist unless the yachts are clearly within two overall lengths of the longer yacht; and an **overlap** which exists between two yachts when the leading yacht **starts,** or when one or both of them completes a **tack** or **gybe,** shall be regarded as a new **overlap** beginning at that time.

3. **Hailing to Stop or Prevent a Luff.** When there is doubt, the **leeward yacht** may assume that she has the right to **luff** unless the helmsman of the **windward yacht** has hailed "Mast Abeam", or words to that effect. The **leeward yacht** shall be governed by such hail, and, if she deems it improper, her only remedy is to protest.

4. **Curtailing a Luff.** The **windward yacht** shall not cause a **luff** to be curtailed because of her proximity to the **leeward yacht** unless an **obstruction,** a third yacht or other object restricts her ability to respond.

5. **Luffing Two or More Yachts.** A yacht shall not **luff** unless she has the right to **luff** all yachts which would be affected by her **luff,** in which case they shall all respond even if an intervening yacht or yachts would not otherwise have the right to **luff.**

39—Sailing Below a Proper Course

A yacht which is on a free leg of the course shall not sail below her **proper course** when she is clearly within three of her overall lengths of either a **leeward yacht** or a yacht **clear astern** which is steering a course to pass to **leeward.**

152 – The Yacht Racing Rules Today

40—Right-of-Way Yacht Luffing before Starting

Before a yacht has **started** and cleared the starting line, any **luff** on her part which causes another yacht to have to alter course to avoid a collision shall be carried out slowly and in such a way as to give the **windward yacht** room and opportunity to keep clear, but the **leeward yacht** shall not so **luff** above a **close-hauled** course, unless the helmsman of the **windward yacht** (sighting abeam from his normal station) is abaft the mainmast of the **leeward yacht**. Rules 38.3, Hailing to Stop or Prevent a Luff; 38.4, Curtailing a Luff; and 38.5, Luffing Two or more Yachts, also apply.

SECTION D—CHANGING TACK RULES

41—Tacking or Gybing

1. A yacht which is either **tacking** or **gybing** shall keep clear of a yacht **on a tack.**

2. A yacht shall neither **tack** nor **gybe** into a position which will give her right of way unless she does so far enough from a yacht **on a tack** to enable this yacht to keep clear without having to begin to alter her course until after the **tack** or **gybe** has been completed.

3. A yacht which **tacks** or **gybes** has the onus of satisfying the race committee that she completed her **tack** or **gybe** in accordance with rule 41.2.

4. When two yachts are both **tacking** or both **gybing** at the same time, the one on the other's **port** side shall keep clear.

SECTION E—RULES OF EXCEPTION AND SPECIAL APPLICATION

When a rule of this section applies, to the extent to which it explicitly provides rights and obligations, it over-rides any conflicting rule of Part IV which precedes it, except the rules of Section A—Rules Which Always Apply.

42—Rounding or Passing Marks and Obstructions

1. **Fundamental Rules Regarding Room.** When yachts either on the same **tack** or, after **starting** and clearing the starting line, on opposite **tacks,** are about to round or pass a **mark** on the same required side, with the exception of a starting **mark** surrounded by navigable water, or an **obstruction** on the same side:—

   (a) When **Overlapped:**
   - (i) An outside yacht shall give each yacht **overlapping** her on the inside, room to round or pass the **mark** or **obstruction,** except as provided in rules 42.1(a)(iii), and (iv) and 42.3. Room includes room for an **overlapping** yacht to **tack** or **gybe** when either is an integral part of the rounding or passing manoeuvre.
   - (ii) When an inside yacht of two or more **overlapped** yachts either on opposite **tacks,** or on the same **tack** without **luffing** rights, will have to **gybe** in order most directly to assume a **proper course** to the next **mark,** she shall **gybe** at the first reasonable opportunity.
   - (iii) When two yachts on opposite **tacks** are on a beat or when one of them will have to **tack** either to round the **mark** or to avoid the **obstruction,** as between each other rule 42.1(a)(i) shall not apply and they are subject to rules 36, Opposite Tack Fundamental Rule, and 41, Tacking or Gybing.
   - (iv) An outside **leeward yacht** with luffing rights may take an inside yacht to windward of a **mark** provided that she hails to that effect and begins to **luff** before she is within two of her overall lengths of the **mark** and provided that she also passes to windward of it.

   (b) When **Clear Astern** and **Clear Ahead:**
   - (i) A yacht **clear astern** shall keep clear in anticipation of and during the rounding or passing manoeuvre

when the yacht **clear ahead** remains on the same **tack** or **gybes.**
  (ii) A yacht **clear ahead** which **tacks** to round a **mark** is subject to rule 41, Tacking or Gybing, but a yacht **clear astern** shall not **luff** above **close-hauled** so as to prevent the yacht **clear ahead** from **tacking.**
2. **Restrictions on Establishing and Maintaining an Overlap**
   (*a*) A yacht **clear astern** shall not establish an inside **overlap** and be entitled to room under rule 42.1(*a*)(i) when the yacht **clear ahead:**—
      (i) is within two of her overall lengths of the **mark** or **obstruction,** except as provided in rules 42.2(*b*) and 42.2(*c*), or
      (ii) is unable to give the required room.
   (*b*) The two-lengths determinative above shall not apply to yachts, of which one has completed a **tack** within two overall lengths of a **mark** or an **obstruction.**
   (*c*) A yacht **clear astern** may establish an **overlap** between the yacht **clear ahead** and a continuing **obstruction** such as a shoal or the shore, only when there is room for her to do so in safety.
   (*d*) (i) A yacht **clear ahead** shall be under no obligation to give room to a yacht **clear astern** before an **overlap** is established.
      (ii) A yacht which claims an inside **overlap** has the onus of satisfying the race committee that the **overlap** was established in proper time.
   (*e*) (i) When an outside yacht is **overlapped** at the time she comes within two of her overall lengths of a **mark** or an **obstruction,** she shall continue to be bound by rule 42.1(*a*)(i) to give room as required even though the **overlap** may thereafter be broken.
      (ii) An outside yacht which claims to have broken an **overlap** has the onus of satisfying the race committee that she became **clear ahead** when she was more than two of her overall lengths from the **mark** or an **obstruction.**

3. At a Starting Mark Surrounded by Navigable Water

When approaching the starting line to **start,** a **leeward yacht** shall be under no obligation to given any **windward yacht** room to pass to leeward of a starting **mark** surrounded by navigable water; but, after the starting signal, a **leeward yacht** shall not deprive a **windward yacht** of room at such a **mark** by sailing either above the course to the first **mark** or above **close-hauled.**

43—Close-Hauled, Hailing for Room to Tack at Obstructions

1. **Hailing.** When two **close-hauled** yachts are on the same **tack** and safe pilotage requires the yacht **clear ahead** or the **leeward yacht** to make a substantial alteration of course to clear an **obstruction,** and if she intends to **tack,** but cannot **tack** without colliding with the other yacht, she shall hail the other yacht for room to **tack** and clear the other yacht, but she shall not hail and **tack** simultaneously.

2. **Responding.** The hailed yacht at the earliest possible moment after the hail shall either:—
   - (*a*) **tack,** in which case, the hailing yacht shall begin to **tack** either:—
     - (i) before the hailed yacht has completed her **tack,** or
     - (ii) if she cannot then **tack** without colliding with the hailed yacht, immediately she is able to **tack** and clear her, or
   - (*b*) reply "You **tack**", or words to that effect, if in her opinion she can keep clear without **tacking** or after postponing her **tack.** In this case:—
     - (i) the hailing yacht shall immediately **tack** and
     - (ii) the hailed yacht shall keep clear.
     - (iii) The onus shall lie on the hailed yacht which replied "You **tack**" to satisfy the race committee that she kept clear.

3. **Limitation on Right to Room when the Obstruction is a Mark.**
   - (*a*) When the hailed yacht can fetch an **obstruction** which is also a **mark,** the hailing yacht shall not be entitled to room to **tack** and clear the other yacht and the hailed

yacht shall immediately so inform the hailing yacht.
- (b) If, thereafter, the hailing yacht again hails for room to **tack** and clear the other yacht she shall, after receiving it, retire immediately.
- (c) If, after having refused to respond to a hail under rule 43.3(a), the hailed yacht fails to fetch, she shall **retire** immediately.

44—Yachts Returning to Start

1. (a) A premature starter when returning to **start,** or a yacht working into position from the course side of the starting line or its extensions, when the starting signal is made, shall keep clear of all yachts which are **starting,** or have **started,** correctly, until she is wholly on the pre-start side of the starting line or its extensions.
   (b) Thereafter, she shall be accorded the rights under the rules of Part IV of a yacht which is **starting** correctly; but if she thereby acquires right of way over another yacht which is **starting** correctly, she shall allow that yacht ample room and opportunity to keep clear.
2. A premature starter while continuing to sail the course and until it is obvious that she is returning to **start,** shall be accorded the rights under the rules of Part IV of a yacht which has **started.**

45—Yachts Re-rounding after Touching a Mark

1. A yacht which has touched a **mark,** and is about to exonerate herself in accordance with rule 52.2, Touching a Mark, shall keep clear of all other yachts which are about to round or pass it or have rounded or passed it correctly, until she has rounded it completely and has cleared it and is on a **proper course** to the next **mark.**

2. A yacht which has touched a **mark** while continuing to sail the course and until it is obvious that she is returning to round it completely in accordance with rule 52.2, Touching a Mark, shall be accorded rights under the rules of Part IV.

SECTION F—WHEN NOT UNDER WAY
46—Anchored, Aground or Capsized

1. A yacht under way shall keep clear of another yacht **racing** which is anchored, aground or capsized. Of two anchored yachts, the one which anchored later shall keep clear, except that a yacht which is dragging shall keep clear of one which is not.

2. A yacht anchored or aground shall indicate the fact to any yacht which may be in danger of fouling her. Unless the size of the yachts or the weather conditions make some other signal necessary, a hail is sufficient indication.

3. A yacht shall not be penalized for fouling a yacht in distress which she is attempting to assist or a yacht which goes aground or capsizes immediately ahead of her.

PART VI—PROTESTS, DISQUALIFICATION AND APPEALS

67—Contact between Yachts Racing

1. When there is contact between the hull, spars, standing rigging or crew of two yachts while racing, both shall be disqualified, unless one of them retires in acknowledgement of an infringement of the rules, or one or both of them acts in accordance with rule 68.3, Protests.

2. A Third yacht which witnesses an apparent collision between two yachts and, after finishing or retiring, discovers that neither of them has observed rule 67.1, is relieved by rule 68.3(b) from the requirement of showing a protest flag and may lodge a protest against them.

3. The race committee may waive this rule when it is satisfied that minor contact was unavoilable.

68—Protests

1. A yacht can protest against any other yacht, except that a protest for an alleged infringement of the rules of Part IV can be

made only by a yacht directly involved in, or witnessing an incident.

2. A protest occurring between yachts competing in separate races sponsored by different clubs shall be heard by a combined committee of the clubs concerned.

3. (*a*) A protest for an infringement of the rules or sailing instructions occurring during a race shall be signified by showing a flag (International Code flag **"B"** is always acceptable, irrespective of any other provisions in the sailing instructions) conspicuously in the rigging of the protesting yacht at the first reasonable opportunity and keeping it flying until she has **finished** or retired, or if the first reasonable opportunity occurs after **finishing,** until acknowledged by the race committee. In the case of a yacht sailed single-handed, it will be sufficient if the flag (whether displayed in the rigging or not) is brought to the notice of the yacht protested against as soon as possible after the incident and to the race committee when the protesting yacht **finishes.**

(*b*) A yacht which has no knowledge of the facts justifying a protest until after she has **finished** or retired may nevertheless protest without having shown a protest flag.

(*c*) A protesting yacht shall try to inform the yacht protested against that a protest will be lodged.

(*d*) Such a protest shall be in writing and be signed by the owner or his representative, and include the following particulars:
  (i) The date, time and whereabouts of the incident.
  (ii) The particular rule or rules or sailing instructions alleged to have been infringed.
  (iii) A statement of the facts.
  (iv) Unless irrelevant, a diagram of the incident.

(*e*) Unless otherwise prescribed in the sailing instructions a protesting yacht shall deliver or, if that is not possible, mail her protest to the race committee:
  (i) within two hours of the time she **finishes** the race

or within such time as may have been prescribed in the sailing instructions under rule 3.2(*b*)(xv), unless the race committee has reason to extend these time limits, or
   (ii) when she does not **finish** the race, within such a time as the race committee may consider reasonable in the circumstances of the case.

   A protest shall be accompanied by such fee, if any, as may have been prescribed in the sailing instructions under rule 3.2(*b*)(xv).
(*f*) The race committee shall allow the protestor to remedy at a later time:
   (i) any defects in the details required by rule 68.3(*d*) provided that the protest includes a summary of the facts, and
   (ii) a failure to deposit such fee as may be required under rule 68.3(*e*) and prescribed in the sailing instructions.
4. (*a*) A protest that a measurement, scantling or flotation rule has been infringed while **racing,** or that a classification or rating certificate is for any reason invalid, shall be lodged with the race committee not later than 18.00 hours on the day following the race. The race committee shall send a copy of the protest to the yacht protested against and, when there appears to be reasonable grounds for the protest, it shall refer the question to an authority qualified to decide such questions.
   (*b*) Deviations in excess of tolerances stated in the class rules caused by normal wear or damage and which do not affect the performance of the yacht shall not invalidate the measurement or rating certificate of the yacht for a particular race, but shall be rectified before she **races** again, unless in the opinion of the race committee there has been no practical opportunity to rectify the wear or damage.
   (*c*) The race committee, in making its decision, shall be gov-

erned by the determination of such authority. Copies of such decision shall be sent to all yachts involved.

5. (a) A yacht which alleges that her chances of winning a prize have been prejudiced by an action or omission of the race committee, may seek redress from the race committee in accordance with the requirements for a protest provided in rules 68.3(*d*), (*e*) and (*f*). In these circumstances a protest flag need not be shown.

(b) When the race committee decides that such action or omission was prejudical, and that the result of the race was altered thereby, it shall **cancel** or **abandon** the race, or make such other arrangement as it deems equitable.

6. A protest made in writing shall not be withdrawn, but shall be decided by the race committee, unless prior to the hearing full responsibility is acknowledged by one or more yachts.

7. Alternative Penalties. When so prescribed in the sailing instructions, the procedure and penalty for infringing a rule of Part IV shall be as provided in Appendix 3, Alternative Penalties for Infringement of a Rule of Part IV.

69—Refusal of a Protest

1. When the race committee decides that a protest does not conform to the requirements of rule 68, Protests, it shall inform the protesting yacht that her protest will not be heard and of the reasons for such decision.

2. Such a decision shall not be reached without giving the protesting yacht an opportunity of bringing evidence that the requirements of rule 68, Protests, were complied with.

70—Hearings

1. When the race committee decides that a protest conforms to all the requirements of rule 68, Protests, it shall call a hearing as soon as possible. The protest, or a copy of it, shall be made available to all yachts involved, and each shall be notified, in writing if practicable, of the time and place set for the hearing. A reasonable time shall be allowed for the preparation of defence. At

the hearing, the race committee shall take the evidence presented by the parties to the protest and such other evidence as it may consider necessary. The parties to the protest, or a representative of each, shall have the right to be present, but all others, except one witness at a time while testifying, may be excluded. A yacht other than one named in the protest, which is involved in that protest, shall have all the rights of yachts originally named in it.

2. A yacht shall not be penalized without a hearing, except as provided in rule 73.1(*a*), Disqualification without Protest.

3. Failure on the part of any of the interested parties or a representative to make an effort to attend the hearing of the protest may justify the race committee in deciding the protest as it thinks fit without a full hearing.

71—Decisions

The race committee shall make its decision promptly after the hearing. Each decision shall be communicated to the parties involved, and shall state fully the facts and grounds on which it is based and shall specify the rules, if any, infringed. If requested by any of the parties, such decision shall be given in writing and shall include the race committee's diagram. The findings of the race committee as to the facts involved shall be final.

72—Disqualification after Protest and Liability for Damages

1. When the race committee, after hearing a protest or acting under rule 73, Disqualification without Protest, or any appeal authority, is satisfied:—
   (*a*) that a yacht has infringed any of these rules or the sailing instructions, or
   (*b*) that in consequence of her neglect of any of these rules or the sailing instructions she has compelled other yachts to infringe any of these rules or the sailing instructions,
she shall be disqualified unless the sailing instructions applicable to that race provide some other penalty. Such disqualification or other penalty shall be imposed, irrespective of whether the rule or sailing instruction which led to the disqualification or penalty was

162 – The Yacht Racing Rules Today

mentioned in the protest, or the yacht which was at fault was mentioned or protested against, e.g., the protesting yacht or a third yacht might be disqualified and the protested yacht absolved.

2. For the purpose of awarding points in a series, a retirement after an infringement of any of these rules or the sailing instructions shall not rank as a disqualification. This penalty can be imposed only in accordance with rules 72, Disqualification after Protest, and 73, Disqualification without Protest.

3. When a yacht either is disqualified or has retired, the next in order shall be awarded her place.

4. The question of damages arising from an infringement of any of these rules or the sailing instructions shall be governed by the prescriptions, if any, of the national authority.

73—Disqualification without Protest

1. (*a*) A yacht which fails either to **start** or to **finish** may be disqualified without protest or hearing, after the conclusion of the race, except that she shall be intitled to a hearing, provided that she satisfies the race committee that an error may have been made.
   (*b*) A yacht so penalized shall be informed of the action taken, either by letter or by notification in the racing results.
2. When the race committee:—
   (*a*) sees an apparent infringement by a yacht of any of these rules or the sailing instructions (except as provided in rule 73.1), or
   (*b*) has reasonable grounds for believing that an infringement resulted in serious damage, or
   (*c*) receives a report not later than the same day from a witness who was neither competing in the race, nor otherwise an interested party, alleging an infringement, or
   (*d*) has reasonable grounds for supposing from the evidence at the hearing of a valid protest, that any yacht involved in the incident may have committed an infringement,

it may notify such yacht thereof orally, or if that is not possible, in writing, delivered or mailed not later than 18.00 hours on the day after:—
      (i) the finish of the race, or
      (ii) the receipt of the report, or
      (iii) the hearing of the protest.

Such notice shall contain a statement of the pertinent facts and of the particular rule or rules or sailing instructions believed to have been infringed, and the race committee shall act thereon in the same manner as if it had been a protest made by a competitor.

74—Penalties for Gross Infringement of Rules

1. When a gross infringement of any of these rules, the sailing instructions or class rules is proved against the owner, the owner's representative, the helmsman or sailing master of a yacht, such persons may be disqualified by the national authority, for any period it may think fit, from either steering or sailing in a yacht in any race held under its jurisdiction.

2. Notice of any penalty adjudged under this rule shall be communicated to the I.Y.R.U. which shall inform all national authorities.

3. After a gross breach of good manners or sportsmanship the race committee may exclude a competitor from further participation in a series or take other disciplinary action.

75—Persons Interested not to take part in Decision

1. No member of either a race committee or of any appeals authority shall take part in the discussion or decision upon any disputed question in which he is an interested party, but this does not preclude him from giving evidence in such a case.

2. The term "interested party" includes anyone who stands to gain or lose as a result of the decision.

76—Expenses Incurred by Protest

Unless otherwise prescribed by the race committee, the fees and expenses entailed by a protest on measurement or classification shall be paid by the unsuccessful party.

77—Appeals

1. Unless otherwise prescribed by the national authority which has recognised the sponsoring organization concerned, an appeal against the decision of a race committee shall be governed by rules 77, Appeals, and 78, Particulars to be Supplied in Appeals.

2. Unless otherwise prescribed by the national authority or in the sailing instructions (subject to rule 2(*j*) or 3.2(*b*)(xvii)), a protest which has been decided by the race committee shall be referred to the national authority solely on a question of interpretation of these rules, within such period after the receipt of the race committee's decision as the national authority may decide:—

   (*a*) when the race committee, at its own instance, thinks proper to do so, or
   (*b*) when any of the parties involved in the protest makes application for such reference.

This reference shall be accompanied by such deposit as the national authority may prescribe, payable by the appellant, to be forfeited to the funds of the national authority in the event of the appeal being dismissed.

3. The national authority shall have power to uphold or reverse the decision of the race committee, and if it is of opinion, from the facts found by the race committee, that a yacht involved in a protest has infringed an applicable rule, it shall disqualify her, irrespective of whether the rule or sailing instruction which led to such disqualification was mentioned in the protest.

4. The decision of the national authority, which shall be final, shall be communicated in writing to all interested parties.

5. (*a*) In the Olympic Regatta and such international regattas as may be specially approved by the I.Y.R.U., the decisions of the jury or judges shall be final.

   (*b*) Other international regattas shall be under the jurisdiction of the national authority of the country in which the regatta is held, and if satisfied that a competent inter-

Appendix A – 165

national jury has been appointed, it may give consent for the decisions of the jury to be final.

6. An appeal once lodged with the national authority shall not be withdrawn.

78—Particulars to be Supplied in Appeals

1. The reference to the national authority shall be in writing and shall contain the following particulars, in order, so far as they are applicable:—
- (a) A copy of the notice of the race and the sailing instructions supplied to the yachts.
- (b) A copy of the protest, or protests, if any, prepared in accordance with rule 68.3(d), and all other written statements which may have been put in by the parties.
- (c) The observations of the race committee thereon, a full statement of the facts found, its decision and the grounds thereof.
- (d) An official digram prepared by the race committee in accordance with the facts found by it, showing:—
    - (i) The course to the next **mark,** or, if close by, the **mark** itself with the required side;
    - (ii) the direction and force of the wind;
    - (iii) the set and strength of the current, if any;
    - (iv) the depth of water, if relevant; and
    - (v) the positions and courses of all the yachts involved.
    - (vi) it is preferable to show yachts sailing from the bottom of the diagram towards the top.
- (e) The grounds of the appeal, to be supplied by either:—
    - (i) the race committee under rule 77.2(a); or
    - (ii) the appellant under rule 77.2(b).
- (f) Observations, if any, upon the appeal by the race committee or any of the parties.

2. The race committee shall notify all parties that an appeal will be lodged and shall invite them to make any observations upon it. Any such observations shall be forwarded with the appeal.

APPENDIX B

Changes in the 1969 Racing Rules, Parts I and IV

In Part I, Definitions, "Starting" says "A yacht **starts** when, after fulfilling her penalty obligations, if any, under rule 51.1(c), Sailing the Course, and, after her starting signal . . ." Rule 51.1(c) is the "one-minute" rule. "Direction of the first **mark**" has been replaced by "direction of the course to the first **mark**."

"Finishing" has an addition: ". . . after fulfilling any penalty obligations, if any, under rule 52.2, Touching a Mark."

In Part IV, Rule 31, Disqualification, now officially permits penalties other than disqualification. It reads: "A yacht may be disqualified *or penalized* for infringing a rule of Part IV . . ." (Italics added.)

Rule 32, Avoiding Collisions, has been changed subtly but significantly. Until now, it has said "A right-of-way yacht which makes *no* attempt to avoid a collision resulting in serious damage may be disqualified as well as the other yacht." Now, it reads "A right-of-way yacht which fails to make a *reasonable* attempt . . ." (Italics added.) Before, making any attempt, no matter how slight, was enough to get a boat-cruncher off the hook. Now, his attempt will need to be considered "reasonable" by the protest committee.

Rule 34 has a new title—Right-of-Way Yacht Altering Course. Although rule 34 obligates a right-of-way boat, it also increases her freedom of movement. Consider this situation: just before the start you, on starboard tack, are reaching along the starting line with plenty of room. A port-tacker approaches; his course is on a line slightly to windward of your position. If neither of you changes course, he will pass to windward of you, thus keeping clear as required. However, you now change to a close-hauled course in order to start. Believe it or not, you would have been vulnerable under old rule 34 in that you changed course in such a way as to obstruct the other boat. Now, you can breathe more easily in such circumstances. There are two exceptions to rule 34; the second one is new, and allows a starboard tack boat to start without fear of this rule.

The remainder of the rule now reads ". . . except:

(a) to the extent permitted by rule 38.1, Right-of-Way Yacht Luffing after Starting, and

(b) when assuming a **proper course** to **start,** unless subject to the second part of rule 44.1(b), Yachts Returning to Start."

Note also the exception to the second exception; if you have returned after a premature start (44.1(b)) and encounter a port-tacker making his start, you must allow him "ample room and opportunity" to keep clear. He must keep clear of you, since you have returned to the right side of the starting line, but you may not obstruct him and then use exception "b" of rule 34 as your defense.

In the old rules, rule 35, Hailing, was a non-rule. It said you "should" hail in certain circumstances, but this was technically only a strongly expressed piece of advice. Now, the "shoulds" have been carefully culled out of the rules ("shall," "can," and "may" are still used and explained in the introductory note), and rule 35 takes on new meaning. The rule is now a rule, with some weight behind it.

The second part of the same rule offers a small reward for hailing, in saying that "A yacht which hails when claiming the establishment or termination of an overlap or insufficiency of room at a **mark** or **obstruction** thereby helps to support her claim for the purposes of rule 42, Rounding or Passing Marks and Obstructions."

Rule 40, Right-of-Way Yacht Luffing before Starting, is now slightly shorter than before—a welcome exception in a longer new rulebook. More important, it makes life on the starting line simpler. The phrase "before her starting signal" has been removed, thereby eliminating the need to distinguish three separate time periods: before the starting signal, between the starting signal and actually starting, and after starting. The second one can now be ignored.

Rule 42 has a new twist; 42.1(a)(ii) not only requires an inside boat on starboard tack which overlaps an outside port tack boat to jibe around a mark; it now makes the same requirement of the inside boat of two boats on the same tack, if the inner boat has no luffing rights under rule 38.1.

Old 42.1(e), called the anti-barging rule, now has its own private number—42.3—and a few words have been added to 42.2(a) for clarity but without even a small change in meaning.

Rule 42.2(b), under "Restrictions on Establishing and Maintaining an Overlap," is now shorter, and clearer, than before. The meaning remains almost the same; it states when the two-length circle can be ignored: "The two-lengths determinative above shall not apply to yachts, of which one has completed a **tack** within two overall lengths of a **mark** or an **obstruction.**" Before, this rule contained an exception to an exception to a condition (the two-length limit) of an exception (rule 42) to the other rules of Part IV excepting those in Section A. Now, it is only an exception to the condition of the exception to the other rules. That's a small step forward.

In the minor changes department, the words "or an **obstruction**" have been added to rules 42.2(b) and 42.2(e)(i) and (ii), since almost all of rule 42 deals with both marks and obstructions. This is not a change in meaning. Also, most all of rule 42, an especially long rule, has been renumbered.

In rule 43, Close-Hauled, Hailing for Room to Tack at Obstructions, "room to **tack**" has been changed in all instances to "room to **tack** and clear" the other yacht. The meaning is unchanged; the extra words are there only for ultra-fine clarity. Also for clarity, 43.3 is now called "Limitation on Right to Room when the Obstruction is a Mark" and is slightly reworded.

The last change in Part IV is in rule 44, Yachts Returning to Start, and changes no meaning. Instead of referring to the wrong side and right side of the starting line, it speaks of the course side and the pre-start side. These new phrases also appear in rule 51, Sailing the Course.

APPENDIX C

The Iceboat Racing Rules

Promulgated by the National Iceboat Authority in the U.S., these rules are in use by all iceboat classes in North America and are also used by the International DN Ice Yacht Racing Association, the only class having any international racing of significance.

Considerably more simple than the IYRU Yacht Racing Rules, the iceboat rules reflect the major differences between hard-water and soft-water racing. Speeds on the ice are between 50 and 100 m.p.h. in most conditions. Races are always conducted on windward-leeward courses with a standing start and downwind finishes. Several laps are sailed, so that mark-roundings are numerous and sometimes crowded. Safety is the prime consideration behind the rules.

Perhaps the most interesting difference is that on the run, when two boats on the same tack are overlapped, the windward boat has right-of-way. This is a safety factor: when a gust hits, bearing off immediately is essential to avoid capsize. Thus the windward boat must be free to turn toward the leeward boat.

Another difference is that there is no two-length determinative at marks; the speeds of the boats make any such provision impossible to use.

Appendix C — 171

Boats sailing to windward have right-of-way over those sailing to leeward, as was true of the yacht racing rules for many years.

Parts I and IV of the iceboat racing rules are reprinted here. If you are interested in the complete rules, write to:

> The National Iceboat Authority
> P.O. Box 40
> Williams Bay, Wis. 53191 U.S.A.

Part I—Definitions

When one of the terms defined in Part I is used in its defined sense in the definitions or rules, it is printed in italic. All definitions rank as rules.

Actual Wind—the natural wind.

Windward-Leeward Course—a course sailed around two *Marks*. An imaginary straight line drawn between the two *Marks* is parallel to the *Actual Wind*.

On-the-Wind—A yacht heading less than 90° from the direction from which the *Actual Wind* is blowing is *On-the-Wind*.

Off-the-Wind—A yacht heading more than 90° from the direction from which the *Actual Wind* is blowing is *Off-the-Wind*.

Starboard Tack—A yacht is on a *Starboard Tack* when the *Actual Wind* is approaching from her right side.

Port Tack—A yacht is on a *Port Tack* when the *Actual Wind* is approaching from her left side.

Windward Yacht and *Leeward Yacht*—When two yachts are on the same tack, the one on the side from which the *Actual Wind* is blowing is the *Windward Yacht*, the other is the *Leeward Yacht*.

Tacking—A yacht is *Tacking* from the moment she is beyond head-to-*Actual Wind* until her mainsail has filled on the other side.

Jibing—A yacht is *Jibing* when, with the *Actual Wind* aft, the foot of her mainsail crosses her centerline until it has filled on the other side.

Obstruction—any object a yacht cannot safely sail over.

Mark—any object which a yacht must round or pass on a required side to properly round the course.

Outside—In rule 8 of the Right-of-Way Rules, any yacht to the right of another yacht is the *Outside* yacht.

Cancellation—A *Cancelled* race is one which cannot thereafter be sailed.

Postponement—A *Postponed* race is one which is not started at its scheduled time and which can be sailed at any time the race committee may direct.

Abandonment—An *Abandoned* race is one which is stopped while it is in progress and which can be re-sailed at the discretion of the race committee.

Part IV—Sailing Rules

Any infraction of the following rules is cause for disqualification.

A. Fair Sailing—In all situations the Judges, Race Committee, and contestants must act in terms of common sense, safety, and good sportsmanship.
B. Right-of-way-Rules.
  1. A yacht in motion shall keep clear of a yacht stopped.
  2. A yacht sailing *Off-the-Wind* shall keep clear of a yacht sailing *On-the-Wind*.
  3. When two yachts are sailing *On-the-Wind*, the yacht on the *Port Tack* shall keep clear of the yacht on the *Starboard Tack*.
  When two yachts are sailing *Off-the-Wind*, the yacht on the *Port Tack* shall keep clear of the yacht on the *Starboard Tack*.
  4. When two yachts sailing *On-the-Wind* are on the same tack, the *Windward Yacht* shall keep clear. When two yachts sailing *Off-the-Wind* are on the same tack, the *Leeward Yacht* shall keep clear.
  5. A right-of-way yacht shall not alter her course so as to mislead or prevent a non-right-of-way yacht from keeping clear. When a faster moving yacht approaches another yacht on the same tack from the rear, the faster yacht must not sail so close that the slower yacht cannot keep clear.
  6. A yacht may not *Tack* or *Jibe* so as to involve the probability of collision with another yacht which, owing to her position or speed, cannot keep clear.

Appendix C – 173

   7. A yacht approaching and unable to clear an *Obstruction* without fouling or endangering another yacht may signal the other yacht for room to clear. The signaled yacht shall at once give room and if it is necessary for her to *Tack* or *Jibe*, the signaling yacht shall also *Tack* or *Jibe* immediately thereafter.
   8. When approaching or rounding a *Mark*, an *Outside* yacht shall keep clear. Each yacht shall be entitled to room to cross the finish line.
   9. After finishing a race, a yacht shall keep clear of the course and yachts still racing.
C. Sailing the Course
   1. A yacht shall be disqualified without protest if she starts prematurely.
   2. A yacht fouling a *Mark* (except when avoiding an accident), not leaving a *Mark* on the required side, or not rounding all *Marks* in proper sequence, shall be disqualified.
D. Propulsion—A yacht may not employ any means of propulsion other than the action of the wind on the sails. However, the crew (unassisted by anyone except for reasons of physical disability as authorized by the Judges) may push the yacht to leave the starting line or to return the yacht to wind propulsion when necessary. Other pushing shall be cause for disqualification.
E. Ballast—A yacht must start and finish a race with the same ballast and crew.

APPENDIX D

Mailing Addresses

The International Yacht Racing Union
  60 Knightsbridge
  London SWIX 7JX
  England

The North American Yacht Racing Union
  1133 Avenue of Americas
  New York, New York 10036
  U.S.A.

The Royal Yachting Association
  Victoria Way
  Woking, Surrey GU21 1EQ
  England

The Canadian Yachting Association
  333 River Road
  Ottawa K1L 8B9
  Canada

APPENDIX E

Rules Numerically Listed

31	107–109, 149		99, 118, 120, 122–123, 125, 151, 168
31.1	108, 149		
31.2	108–109, 149	**38.2**	58, 70, 118, 151
32	107, 109–110, 149, 166–167	**38.3**	32, 61–62, 66–67, 116, 123, 151
33	107, 109, 110, 149		
34	23–24, 26, 34, 54, 65, 97–102, 104, 118, 120, 122, 126, 127, 149, 167	**38.4**	62–64, 66–67, 151
		38.5	64, 66–67, 151
		39	36, 42, 48–53, 65, 122, 123, 151
34(a)	150		
34(b)	102, 150	**40**	42, 55, 66, 89, 97, 115, 118, 152, 168
35	23, 24, 26, 32, 54, 102–103, 123, 125, 150, 167–168		
		41	32, 37–38, 100, 126, 152
35.1	34, 109, 150	**41.1**	31, 38–40, 70, 101, 104, 114, 152
35.2	103, 127, 150		
36	9, 25, 26, 28, 31, 32, 35, 73, 99, 114, 115, 119, 120, 126, 127, 150	**41.2**	23, 24, 25–26, 27, 31, 32, 40, 41, 114, 119, 136, 152
		41.3	40, 119, 152
37	36, 122, 123, 124, 150	**41.4**	103–104, 152
37.1	15–18, 26, 27, 28, 41, 42, 45, 51, 52–54, 55, 62, 69, 73, 75, 85, 86, 89, 115, 119, 120, 121, 123, 125, 128, 150	**42**	20–23, 32, 33, 69, 75, 76, 79, 83–84, 85–86, 124, 127, 128, 153–155, 168, 169
		42.1	70–73, 82, 153–154
		42.1(a)	153
37.2	18–20, 26, 27, 41, 42, 52, 53, 55, 75, 79, 115, 119, 150	**42.1(a)(i)**	26, 42, 68–69, 75, 76–77, 82, 84, 89, 90, 92, 123, 128, 153
		42.1(a)(ii)	73–75, 153, 168
37.3	32, 43–45, 46–47, 52, 53, 55, 115, 116, 122–123, 150	**42.1(a)(iii)**	75, 83, 153
		42.1(a)(iv)	79–83, 125, 153
38	33, 42, 54–55, 65, 82, 97, 101, 117–118, 120, 122, 123, 124, 151	**42.1(b)**	153–154
		42.1(b)(i)	34, 42, 75, 153–154
38.1	55–58, 64, 65, 75, 82–83, 86,	**42.1(b)(ii)**	75, 87, 154

175

176 – The Yacht Racing Rules Today

42.1(e)	168	68.3(a)	158
42.2	154	68.3(b)	111, 158
42.2(a)	154, 168	68.3(c)	132, 158
42.2(a)(i)	76, 86, 154	68.3(d)	158
42.2(a)(ii)	32, 76, 83, 154	68.3(d)(i)	158
42.2(b)	84–85, 121, 154, 168, 169	68.3(d)(ii)	158
42.2(c)	34, 83, 96, 154	68.3(d)(iii)	158
42.2(d)	154	68.3(d)(iv)	158
42.2(d)(i)	32, 77–78, 154	68.3(e)	158–159
42.2(d)(ii)	78, 154	68.3(e)(i)	134, 158–159
42.2(e)	83, 154	68.3(e)(ii)	159
42.2(e)(i)	78, 154, 169	68.3(f)	142, 159
42.2(e)(ii)	78, 125, 154, 169	68.3(f)(i)	159
42.3	88–89, 90, 155, 116–117, 168	68.3(f)(ii)	159
		68.4(a)	159
43	32, 89, 90, 92–93, 128, 155–156, 169	68.4(b)	159
		68.4(c)	159–160
43.1	92, 155	68.5	138, 160
43.2	91–92, 93, 155	68.5(a)	138, 160
43.2(a)	155	68.5(b)	160
43.2(a)(i)	155	68.6	134–140, 160
43.2(a)(ii)	155	68.7	160
43.2(b)	155	69	135, 142, 160
43.2(b)(i)	155	69.1	160
43.2(b)(ii)	155	69.2	160
43.2(b)(iii)	155	70	134, 135, 137, 160–161
43.3	94, 117, 155–156, 169	70.1	160–161
43.3(a)	155–156	70.2	161
43.3(b)	109, 117, 156	70.3	137, 161
43.3(c)	109, 156	71	140, 161
44	33, 104, 106, 156, 169	72	161–162
44.1(a)	104–105, 156	72.1	134, 137, 161–162
44.1(b)	32, 105, 150, 156	72.1(a)	161
44.2	105–106, 156	72.1(b)	139–140, 161–162
45	33, 104, 106, 156	72.2	162
45.1	156	72.3	162
45.2	156	72.4	162
46	157	73	135, 162–163
46.1	157	73.1(a)	162
46.2	32, 157	73.1(b)	162
46.3	109, 157	73.2	111, 138, 162–163
49	119	73.2(a)	162
51	169	73.2(b)	162
51.1(c)	115, 147	73.2(c)	162
58	107	73.2(d)	162–163
67	110–111, 113, 157	73.2(d)(i)	163
67.1	111, 157	73.2(d)(ii)	163
67.2	157	73.2(d)(iii)	163
67.3	157	74	163
68	157–160	74.1	163
68.1	157–158	74.2	163
68.2	158	74.3	163
68.3	110, 131–132, 158–159		

75	137, 163	**78.1(a)**	165
75.1	163	**78.1(b)**	165
75.2	163	**78.1(c)**	165
76	163–164	**78.1(d)**	165
77	140, 164–165	**78.1(d)(i)**	165
77.1	164	**78.1(d)(ii)**	165
77.2	164	**78.1(d)(iii)**	165
77.2(a)	164	**78.1(d)(iv)**	165
77.2(b)	141, 164	**78.1(d)(v)**	165
77.3	164	**78.1(d)(vi)**	165
77.4	164	**78.1(e)**	165
77.5(a)	164	**78.1(e)(i)**	165
77.5(b)	164–165	**78.1(e)(ii)**	165
77.6	165	**78.1(f)**	165
78	140, 165	**78.2**	140, 169
78.1	165	**78.8**	141

INDEX

Abandoned race, 147, 149
  rule 68.5(b), 160
Aground (rule 46), 106–107, 157
Anchored (rule 46), 106, 107, 157
Appeals (rule 77), 140, 141, 164–165
  rule 77.2(b), 141
  particulars to be supplied in (rule 78), 140, 165
    rule 78.2, 140
    rule 78.8, 141
Australian Yachting Federation, 143
Bearing away, 46, 147, 148
Before the start tactics, 114–118
Borne away, 147
Canadian Yachting Association, 5, 143
Cancelled race, 147, 148
  rule 68.5(b), 160
Capsized (rule 46), 106–107, 157
Changing tack (rule 41), 37–42, 152
  rule 41.1, 38, 70, 152
  rule 41.2, 23, 40, 152
  rule 41.3, 40, 152
  rule 41.4, 103–104, 152
Clear ahead, 147–148
  hailing (rule 43.1), 90–91, 155
  luffing rights (rule 38.1), 55, 151
  overlap, restrictions on (rule 42.2):
    rule 42.2(a)(i), 76, 154
    rule 42.2(c), 96, 154
    rule 42.2(d)(i), 77–78, 154
    rule 42.2(e)(ii), 154
  room, rules regarding (rule 42.1(b)), 153–154
    rule 42.1(b)(i), 22–23, 75
    rule 42.1(b)(ii), 87, 154
  same tack (rule 37.2), 18–20, 42, 150
Clear astern, 71, 147–148
  overlap, restrictions on (rule 42.2):
    rule 42.2(a), 154
    rule 42.2(c), 96, 154
    rule 42.2(d)(i), 77–78, 154
  room, rules regarding (42.1):
    rule 42.1(b), 153–154

    rule 42.1(b)(i), 22–23, 75, 153–154
    rule 42.1(b)(ii), 87, 154
  sailing below a proper course (rule 39), 48–53, 151
  same tack (rule 37):
    rule 37.2, 18–20, 42, 150
    rule 37.3, 43–45, 150
Close-hauled, 147
  hailing for room to tack at obstructions (rule 43), 155–156, 169
    rule 43.1, 90–91
  right-of-way yacht luffing before starting (rule 40), 66, 152
  rounding or passing marks and obstructions (rule 42.1(b)(ii)), 87, 154
  at starting mark (rule 42.3), 88–89, 155
Collisions, avoiding (rule 32), 149, 166–167
Course, changing, 97–104
Damages, liability for, disqualification after (rule 72), 161–162
Decisions (rule 71), 140, 141, 161
  interested party not to take part in, (rule 75), 163
Disqualification (rule 31), 107–109, 149, 166
  after protest and liability for damages (rule 72), 161–162
    rule 72.1(b), 139–140
  without protest (rule 73), 135, 162–163
    rule 73.2, 138
Errors, correcting, 104–106
Finishing, 46, 147, 148
  disqualification (rule 73.1(a)), 162
  protests (rule 68.3)
    rule 68.3(a), 158
    rule 68.3(b), 158
    rule 68.3(e)(i), 158–159

rule 68.3(e)(ii), 159
  tactics, 128
Hailing (rule 35), 102–103, 150, 167–168
  leeward mark tactics, 125
  the reach tactics, 123
  for room to tack at obstructions,
    close-hauled (rule 43), 155–156
    rule 43.1, 90–91, 93
  to stop or prevent a luff (rule 38.3),
    61–62, 66–67, 116, 123, 151
  windward leg tactics, 118–119, 120
Hearings, 134–140
  rule 70, 134, 135, 136, 160–161
  rule 70.3, 137
Iceboat racing rules, 170–173
Interested party (rule 75), 137, 163
International Yacht Racing Union
    (IYRU), 2, 4, 7
  Case 3, 64
  Case 5, 78–79
  Case 6, 139
  Case 10, 100
  Case 11, 47
  Case 23, 30
  Case 25, 47
  Case 35, 98–99
  Case 40, 69–70
  Case 46, 44, 45
  Case 52, 99–100
  Case 53, 32, 109–110
  Case 55, 82
  Racing Rules Committee, 4
Jibing, 147
  changing (rule 41), 126, 127, 152
    rule 41.1, 38–40, 70, 152
    rule 41.2, 23, 40, 41, 152
    rule 41.3, 40, 152
    rule 41.4, 103–104, 152
  right-of-way yacht luffing after
    starting (rule 38.2), 58–61, 151
  room, rules regarding (rule 42.1):
    rule 42.1(a)(i), 69, 153
    rule 42.1(a)(ii), 73–75
    rule 42.1(b)(i), 75, 154
  tactics, 123–124, 126, 127
"Keep clear," defined, 13, 37
Leeward, 34, 148
  sailing below a proper course (rule
    39), 48–53, 151
  same tack (rule 37.3), 150
Leeward mark tactics:
  from the reach, 124–126
  from the run, 127–128

Leeward yacht, 148
  hailing (rule 43.1), 90–91, 155
  right-of-way yacht luffing after
    starting (rule 38):
    rule 38.1, 55, 151
    rule 38.3, 61–62, 151
    rule 38.4, 63–64, 151
  right-of-way yacht luffing before
    starting (rule 40), 66, 152
  room, rules regarding (rule 42.1(a)
    (iv)), 79–83, 153
  sailing below a proper course (rule
    39), 48–53, 151
  same tack (rule 37):
    rule 37.1, 15–18, 150
    rule 37.3, 43–45, 46, 150
  at starting mark (rule 42.3), 88–89,
    155
Luffing, 46, 147, 148
  after starting (rule 38), 42, 55, 82, 97,
    101, 117–118, 151
    rule 38.1, 47, 65, 82, 102–103,
      120, 121, 122, 125, 151
    rule 38.3, 61–62, 116, 151
    rule 38.4, 63–64, 151
    rule 38.5, 64, 66–67, 151
  before starting (rule 40), 42, 47, 66,
    89, 97, 115, 116, 118, 152, 168
  rights, special, 64–67
  room, rules regarding (rule 42.1):
    rule 42.1(a)(ii), 73–75, 153
    rule 42.1(a)(iv), 79–83, 153
    rule 42.1(b)(ii), 87, 154
  tactics:
    before starting, 116–118
    leeward mark, from the reach,
      124–126
    the reach, 122–123
    windward leg, 120
Mark, 147, 148, 166
  appeals (rule 78.1(d)(i)), 165
  hailing (rule 35.2), 103, 150, 168
  leeward, tactics, 124–128
  off the wind, 68–83
  rerounding after touching (rule 45),
    156
    rule 45.1, 106, 156
    rule 45.2, 106, 156
  rounding or passing (rule 42), 13–15,
    20–23, 153–155
    rule 42.1, 88
    rule 42.1(a)(i), 42, 68–69, 76, 153
    rule 42.1(a)(ii), 75, 153

180 — Index

rule 42.1(a)(iii), 153
rule 42.1(a)(iv), 79–83, 153
rule 42.1(b)(i), 34
rule 42.1(b)(ii), 87, 154
rule 42.2(a)(i), 154
rule 42.2(b), 84–85, 154
rule 42.2(e)(i), 78, 154
rule 42.2(e)(ii), 154
rule 42.3, 88–89, 90, 155
starting, 88–90
when also an obstruction (rule 43.3), 94–95, 155–156
windward, 83–87
New Zealand Yachting Federation, 143
North American Yacht Racing Union (NAYRU), 2, 4–5, 7, 143
Case 6, 48
Case 11, 139
Case 20, 64–65
Case 32, 35
Case 36, 44, 89–90
Case 50, 41
Case 53, 77
Case 57, 81
Case 58, 82
Case 63, 100–101
Case 67, 30
Case 74, 53
Case 78, 62
Case 81, 93
Case 87, 78–79
Case 88, 134
Case 104, 137
Case 111, 138
Case 124, 137
Case 126, 44
Case 127, 53
Case 137, 36
Case 142, 139
Case 145, 82
Case 147, 93
Case 151, 62
Obstruction, 95–96, 148
close-hauled, hailing for room to tack at (rule 43), 90–95, 155–156
rule 43.1, 90–91, 92, 155
rule 43.3, 94–95, 155–156
rule 43.3(a), 155
luffing after starting (rule 38.4), 63–64
rounding or passing (rule 42), 20–23, 127, 128, 153–155
rule 42.1(a)(i), 68–69, 76, 90, 123, 125, 153

rule 42.1(a)(iii), 153
rule 42.2(a)(i), 76, 154
rule 42.2(b), 84–85, 154
rule 42.2(c), 34, 96, 154
rule 42.2(e)(i), 78, 154
rule 42.2(e)(ii), 154
On a tack, 34, 147
rule 41.1, 38
rule 41.2, 40, 152
Opposite tack (rule 36), 9–15, 25, 33, 150
Overlapping, 71–73, 147–148
hailing (rule 35.2), 103, 150, 168
luffing after starting (rule 38), 55
rule 38.1, 123–124
rule 38.2, 58–61, 118, 151
restrictions on establishing and maintaining (rule 42.2), 154
rule 42.2(a), 154
rule 42.2(a)(i), 154
rule 42.2(a)(ii), 154
rule 42.2(b), 154
rule 42.2(c), 154
rule 42.2(d)(i), 77–78, 154
rule 42.2(d)(ii), 154
rule 42.2(e)(i), 78, 154
rule 42.2(e)(ii), 125, 154
rounding or passing marks and obstructions when (rule 42.1(a)), 20–23, 34, 153
rule 42.1(a)(i), 68–69, 153
rule 42.1(a)(ii), 73–75, 123, 153
rule 42.1(a)(iii), 153
rule 42.1(a)(iv), 153
same tack (rule 37.3), 36, 43–45, 46, 116, 123, 150
tactics:
  at the finish, 128
  at the jibing mark, 123–124
  leeward mark, 125, 127
Penalties, for gross infringement of rules (rule 74), 163
Penalty system, 129–142
after hearing, 140–141
the hearing, 134–140
rights, 141–142
on shore, 133–134
on the water, 131–133
Port-tack (rule 36), 9–15, 26, 27, 31, 150
Postponed race, 147, 148–149
Proper course, 51–52, 148
rerounding after touching mark (rule 45.1), 106, 156

Index — 181

right-of-way yacht altering course
  (rule 34), 97–102
  rule 34(b), 102, 150, 167
right-of-way yacht luffing after
  starting (rule 38), 55
rounding or passing marks and
  obstructions (rule 42.1(a)(ii)), 73–75, 153
sailing below a (rule 39), 48–53, 151
same tack (rule 37.3), 46–47, 150
Protest flag, 131–133
Protests (rule 68), 110–111, 157–160
  rule 68.3, 131–132, 158–159
  rule 68.3(c), 132–133, 158
  rule 68.3(e)(i), 134, 158–159
  rule 68.5, 138, 160
  rule 68.5(a), 138, 160
  disqualification after (rule 72), 161–162
    rule 72.1, 134, 161–162
  expenses incurred by (rule 76), 163–164
  hearings (rule 70), 141
  refusal of (rule 69), 160
Racing, 108, 147
  anchored, aground or capsized (rule 46.1), 106, 107, 157
  contact between yachts (rule 67), 157
  disqualification (rule 31):
    rule 31.1, 108, 149
    rule 31.2, 108, 149
  protests (rule 68.4):
    rule 68.4(a), 159
    rule 68.4(b), 159
  retiring from race (rule 33), 110, 149
Reach, the, tactics, 122–123
Responding (rule 43.2), 91, 155
Retiring (rule 43.3(c)), 156
Room:
  fundamental rules regarding (rule 42.1), 153–154
  to tack at obstructions (rule 43), 90 95, 155 156
    rule 43.3, 94–95, 155–156
Royal Yachting Association (RYA), 2, 5, 7, 143
  Case 62/37, 139
  Case 63/1, 62, 138
  Case 63/22, 139
  Case 64/26, 93, 132
  Case 65/1, 35–36
  Case 65/9, 36
  Case 65/15, 93

Case 66/10, 77
Case 67/7, 30, 31–32
Case 69/9, 104
Case 72/2, P, 98
Case 73/4, 74
Rule-making process, 4–5
Rules:
  changes in, 166–169
  language of, 5
  numerically listed, see Appendix E
Run, the, tactics, 126–127
Same tack (rule 37), 15–20, 42–56, 121, 122, 150–152
  overlapped, 46–54
  preliminaries, 42–45
  special luffing rights, 54–56
Stalling, holding position by, 115
Starting, 147, 166
  before, tactics, 114–118
  disqualification (rule 73.1(a)), 162
  right-of-way yacht altering course
    (rule 34(b)), 97–102, 150, 167
  right-of-way yacht luffing after (rule 38), 54–55
    rule 38.1, 151
    rule 38.2, 58–61, 151
  right-of-way yacht luffing before (rule 40), 66, 152
  rounding or passing marks and
    obstructions (rule 42):
    rule 42.1, 153
    rule 42.3, 88–89, 155
  yachts returning to (rule 44), 156, 169
    rule 44.1(a), 104–105, 156
    rule 44.1(b), 105, 156
    rule 44.2, 105–106, 156
Starting marks (rule 42.3), 88–90, 155
Tacking, 41, 147, 148
  changing (rule 41), 37–42, 152
    rule 41.1, 38, 70, 152
    rule 41.2, 23, 40, 152
    rule 41.3, 40, 152
    rule 41.4, 103–104, 152
  at obstructions, close-hauled, hailing
    for room (rule 43), 90–95, 155–156
    rule 43.1, 90–91, 155
    rule 43.2, 91–92
    rule 43.2(a), 155
    rule 43.2(a)(i), 155
    rule 43.2(a)(ii), 155
    rule 43.2(b), 155
    rule 43.2(b)(i), 155

rule 43.2(b)(ii), 155
rule 43.3(a), 155, 169
rule 43.3(b), 156, 169
opposite (rule 36), 9–15, 25, 33, 150
right-of-way yacht luffing after starting (rule 38.2), 58–61, 151
rounding or passing marks and obstructions (rule 42):
    rule 42.1, 128, 153
    rule 42.1(a)(i), 69, 153
    rule 42.1(a)(ii), 73–75, 153
    rule 42.1(a)(iii), 75, 153
    rule 42.1(b)(i), 75, 154
    rule 42.1(b)(ii), 75, 87, 154
    rule 42.2(b), 84–85, 121, 154
same (rule 37), 15–20, 42–56, 121, 122, 150–152
    overlapped, 46–54
    preliminaries, 42–45
    special luffing rights, 54–56
starboard (rule 36), 9–15, 26, 27, 150
tactics:
    before the start, 114–118
    at the finish, 128
    at jibing mark, 123–124
    leeward mark, 125
    the reach, 122–123
    the run, 126–127
    at weather mark, 121–122
    windward leg, 118–120
Tactics, 112–128
Weather marks, tactics, 121–122
When not under way (rule 46), 106–107, 157
Windward, 34, 148
Windward leg tactics, 118–120
Windward marks, 83–87
Windward yacht, 148
  right-of-way yacht luffing after starting (rule 38), 55
    rule 38.1, 151
    rule 38.3, 61–62, 151
    rule 38.4, 63–64, 151
  right-of-way yacht luffing before starting (rule 40), 66, 152
  rounding or passing marks and obstructions (rule 42.3), 88–89, 155
  same tack (rule 37):
    rule 37.1, 15–18, 150
    rule 37.3, 43–45, 150